National 5 and Higher ENGLISH for CfE

SCOTTISH SHORT TEXTS

Carolyn Cunningham and Willie McGuire

HODDER GIBSON
AN HACHETTE UK COMPANY

The Publishers would like to thank the following for permission to reproduce copyright material:

Photo credits

p.22 © Gray wall studio – Fotolia.com; p.35 © David Cheskin/ PA Archive/Press Association Images; p.57 © MaZiKab – Fotolia.com; p.65 © Dan Tuffs/REX; p.67 ©TopFoto; p.76 © IWM/Getty Images; p.78 © Stephen Spreadbury – Fotolia.com; p.94 © annavaczi – Fotolia.com; p.106 © Gordon Wright; p.116 © Greg Skomal / NOAA Fisheries Service; p.123 Tyler Olson – Fotolia.com; p.131 © Joseph Reid / Alamy; p.134 © rofus – Fotolia.com; p.142 © alesikka – Fotolia.com.

Chapter opener image reproduced on pages 1, 2, 5, 35, 63, 65, 106, 146 and 164 © ra2 studio – Fotolia.

Acknowledgements

The extract from 'Away in a Manger' is taken from *Hieroglyphics and Other Stories* by Anne Donovan, reproduced by permission of Canongate Books Ltd; Extracts from 'In the Snack-bar', 'Good Friday', 'Trio', 'Winter', 'Slate' and 'Hyena' from *Collected Poems* by Edwin Morgan are reproduced by permission of Carcanet Press Limited, 1996; The extracts from 'The Telegram', 'Mother and Son', 'The Painter' and 'The Red Door' are taken from *The Red Door* by Iain Crichton Smith, reproduced by permission of Birlinn Ltd (www.birlinn.co.uk); Extracts from 'Assisi', 'Basking Shark', 'Visiting Hour', 'Sounds of the Day' and 'Memorial' from *The Poems of Norman MacCaig* by Norman MacCaig are reproduced by permission of Polygon, an imprint of Birlinn Ltd (www.birlinn.co.uk).

Material in Chapter 2: Edwin Morgan has been repurposed from 'Scottish Texts: The Poetry of Edwin Morgan', originally written by Willie McGuire for Education Scotland, 2013, and is reproduced under the terms of the Open Government Licence (http://www.nationalarchives.gov.uk/doc/open-government-licence/).

The critical essay marking grids on pages 164 – 167 are taken from the SQA Specimen Question Papers for National 5 and Higher English, Copyright © Scottish Qualifications Authority.

Every effort has been made to trace all copyright holders, but if any have been inadvertently overlooked the Publishers will be pleased to make the necessary arrangements at the first opportunity.

Although every effort has been made to ensure that website addresses are correct at time of going to press, Hodder Gibson cannot be held responsible for the content of any website mentioned in this book. It is sometimes possible to find a relocated web page by typing in the address of the home page for a website in the URL window of your browser.

Orders: please contact Bookpoint Ltd, 130 Park Drive, Abingdon, Oxon OX14 4SE. Telephone: (44) 01235 827720. Fax: (44) 01235 400454. Lines are open 9.00–5.00, Monday to Saturday, with a 24-hour message answering service. Visit our website at www.hoddereducation.co.uk. Hodder Gibson can be contacted direct on: Tel: 0141 848 1609; Fax: 0141 889 6315; email: hoddergibson@hodder.co.uk

First published in 2014 by

Hodder Gibson, an imprint of Hodder Education,

An Hachette UK Company,

2a Christie Street

Paisley PA1 1NB

Impression number   5   4   3   2   1

Year   2018   2017   2016   2015   2014

Cover photo © ra2 studio – Fotolia

Illustrations by Barking Dog Art Design and Illustration

Typeset in Minion Regular 12/14.5 by Integra Software Services Pvt. Ltd., Pondicherry, India

Printed in Spain

A catalogue record for this title is available from the British Library

ISBN: 978 1 4718 3744 9

CONTENTS

INTRODUCTION

Part 1 contains the National 5 texts, while Part 2 deals with those texts that can be dealt with at either National 5 or Higher levels.

The introduction to each part leads you through the critical reading demands of the National 5 examination. Each of the chapters following this will take you through activities to prepare you for both the Scottish Text and Critical Essay responses. Chapters 1 and 2 take you through a selection of the authors and set texts for National 5 only, while Chapters 3 and 4 cover two writers suitable for both National 5 and Higher. What you may notice, is that the support given reduces as you work your way through each of the chapters. Finally, Chapter 5 provides sample critical essays on each author, with expert commentaries, allowing you to measure your own work against 'very good' examples at National 5 and Higher levels.

INTRODUCTION
WHAT DO I NEED TO KNOW ABOUT NATIONAL 5?

The authors of this book aim to support both teachers and students towards successful outcomes in the Critical Reading elements of National 5 English: Scottish Texts and Critical Essays. To achieve this, students are encouraged to work collaboratively and actively at the outset of tasks while working towards independence as the activities progress.

Critical Reading has the largest number of marks in the examination at 40 marks, while the Reading for Understanding, Analysis and Evaluation section is worth 30 marks and the Writing Portfolio 30 marks. It is, therefore, well worth studying hard in critical reading as it can substantially affect your overall grade.

There are also no surprises in the area of critical reading. The critical essay will be drawn from poetry, prose, drama, film and television drama, or language, while the set texts will be known to you. The only problem is that you don't know which one of the six set texts for each author featured in this textbook, will be chosen for the examination. That is the reason for this book!

In the examination, you must write a critical essay (20 marks) and analyse a Scottish text (20 marks). You are advised by SQA to spend approximately 45 minutes on each. You cannot answer on the same genre in both questions. **Don't** be tempted to spend much longer on any single part. The usual result of this is that one of your pieces is fairly good, although not as good as you might have expected, while the other is very weak as you have not planned your approach properly. There is a range of skills involved in critical essay writing and Scottish text analysis. This book will cover the key skills, one of which is timing. Remember 45 minutes each; no more!

Remember, too, that Norman MacCaig and Iain Crichton Smith are both studied at Higher as well as at National 5. This may be of particular interest to students who are planning for Higher following National 5.

To be successful in the examination, you must do your best with the interactive parts of the book where you are asked to complete activities.

This textbook will prepare you, thoroughly, for the demands of the examination.

This is vital.

Good luck!

The Scottish text questions

These are the first questions to appear on the paper. They are in three areas: drama, prose and poetry. You are also given page numbers for each so that you can find your particular Scottish text quickly. Do find your text quickly as you need to use all of the time in the examination efficiently. As this book concerns itself only with the shorter Scottish texts, the first area to be covered will be prose.

Prose

Prose questions will contain (roughly) a 30-line extract. This can come from anywhere in the text: beginning, middle or end. You are asked to read the extract then answer (usually) five questions, worth 20 marks in total.

Questions 1–4 will usually be about the extract itself and will be worth 12 marks, with the other 8 marks available for the final question. This requires you to relate a key aspect(s) of the extract to at least one other short story by the same author and to make a general comment (determined by the question) on a point of commonality between the texts. This leaves you with the question of whether to select **one** or **more** additional texts and this would depend on the question you are answering, **but do not rule out answering on more than one additional text.**

Poetry

Poetry questions will contain (roughly) a 30-line extract. This will usually be the whole poem. You are asked to read this and then answer (usually) five questions, worth 20 marks.

Questions 1–4 will usually be about the extract itself and will be worth 12 marks, with the other 8 marks available for the final question in which you have to relate a key aspect(s) of the extract to at least one other poem by the same poet. Again, you are left with the decision of whether to select one or more additional texts. The answer to this question should depend on the nature of the question and the content of the texts you have studied. It is better to know all of your texts than to depend on knowledge of only some of them, which is a very risky approach! There are no real shortcuts other than to know your texts well.

The critical essays

In this part of the paper, you have to write a critical essay on either: drama, prose, poetry, film and television drama, or language.

You cannot answer on the same genre as you did in section 1 of the paper. So, if you answered on poetry in section 1, you must answer on either drama, prose, film and television drama, or language in the critical essay. You would be answering on a Scottish text for the critical essay only if you have studied more than one text/author from the list. You are advised to spend 45 minutes on this part of the paper. **No longer!**

Tip 1!

You can answer the paper in any order you choose. You can do the critical essay first.

First find your genre, then a suitable question under that heading.

Tip 2!

It is better not to mix the genres up as you may incur a penalty! Always double and triple check your genre! This means that you must answer on the genre named in the question. You are given guidance as to how to approach the question. In prose, answers to questions should refer to the text and to such relevant features as characterisation, setting, language, key incident(s), climax, turning point, plot, structure, narrative technique, theme, ideas, description …

There are two questions per genre and you only have to write ONE essay, so there are lots of choices.

Note that the ellipsis (…) is there to suggest that you could also make reference to other relevant features. Those listed above are merely there to guide you through the early (frightening) stages of the examination where students can sometimes 'go blank'. Use the pertinent technical features of the text you are going to use.

In poetry, answers should refer to the text and to such relevant features as word choice, tone, imagery, structure, content, rhythm, rhyme, theme, sound, ideas …

Again, note the ellipsis!

Tip 3!

Item writers who produce the critical essay examination papers do not know which text you are going to write about. It may be another Scottish text or it may not, yet you should be able to answer a question on a text you have studied. The questions, therefore, tend to be fairly general. This is good news, but it can also present problems, like when you try to memorise an essay. Not a good idea! We will cover more successful approaches later in the book.

CHAPTER 1
ANNE DONOVAN

Introduction

Anne Donovan had been an English teacher for many years when she attended an Arvon Foundation writing course in 1995, where she was tutored by A.L. Kennedy and Bill Herbert. The publication of *Hieroglyphics* marked a turning point in her career, partly because it was written in Scots. This led the way to considerable success, including the publication of two novels: *Buddha Da* and *Being Emily*.

Take a closer look

See the writer herself on YouTube:

http://tinyurl.com/m2pjk99

What's the story?

If you are studying Anne Donovan for your National 5 Scottish text question, you will read six short stories from the *Hieroglyphics* collection – 'A Chitterin Bite', 'All that Glisters', 'Away in a Manger', 'Dear Santa', 'Virtual Pals' and 'Zimmerobics'. You could, of course, use one of these as a critical essay as opposed to a textual analysis question, but you couldn't do both.

For the Scottish text question in your National 5 exam, you will need to:

- know the individual stories well
- develop your skills in analysis
- make connections between the stories.

Then, on the day of the exam, you will use your knowledge and skills to answer questions on an extract from one of the six stories above. The six stories are all set in Glasgow, and can be grouped together under the following headings:

Relationship	Text(s)
Child–adult	'A Chitterin Bite'
	'All that Glisters'
	'Away in a Manger'
	'Dear Santa'
Child–child	'Virtual pals'
Adult–adult	'Zimmerobics' (where the former child has become the adult figure)

'A Chitterin Bite'

Stage 1: Gaining confident knowledge of the story

The first important thing to do is consolidate your knowledge of the story to make sure you know it, confidently. To achieve this, we will divide the story up into different elements: plot, characters and theme, and we will analyse the writer's style used to create all of these.

The title of this story refers, in Scots, to the piece of bread (sandwich) that you eat when you have been for a swim and need to get warmed up, to stop you chittering with the cold.

Plot summary

1. A young Mary goes to the swimming baths with Agnes, her friend.
2. Afterwards, they go to a café followed by the cinema where they meet two boys.
3. An older Mary goes swimming then meets her married lover, Matthew, at a restaurant.
4. Prior to the meeting, she has given him a love bite that has been spotted by his wife and he and Mary split at the end of the story.

Identify where these quotations are located in the story and explain their function.
The first one is done for you.

Quotation	Where?/Function?
'We'd go tae the baths every Saturday mornin, Agnes and me.'	At the start of the story. Sets the scene. Introduces two of the main characters. Introduces setting through use of Scots and through word choice, 'baths'.
'Inside were two jammy pieces … a chitterin bite.'	
'I still go swimming, but now to the warm and brightly lit leisure centre …'	
'I just broke the last rule.'	
'We never spoke aboot it, Agnes and me … a cauldness grew between us …'	

Structure

The setting alternates between the past and the present, between the young Mary in parts 1 and 2 (in the plot summary on page 6), to the adult Mary in parts 3 and 4.

Task

1. Write down the main events under the headings past and present. Now add the quotations below under the correct heading in the table.

   'ceilin high and pointy like a chapel roof'

   'place is fulla weans, screechin ower the racket'

   'screechin at their pals ower the racket'

   'the shock of the cauld makin us scream'

   'shampoo, conditioner and body lotion tucked neatly in my designer sportsbag'

   'saunas and steam rooms, aromatherapy massages and hot showers'

   'warm and brightly lit leisure centre'

Past	Present

2. Place each of the quotations in the correct column of the table below.

   'anonymous place tucked away in a side street'

   'smell of chips and the steam risin'

   'at our usual table'

   'pinkish glow of the candlelight'

   'booths wi gless panels, frosted like sugar icing'

   'windaes are aye steamed up'

   'the seats flip up and doon on creaky metal hinges'

   'we are unlikely to be spotted here'

Café	Restaurant

Story shapes

Stories can be shaped like this:

Beginning   middle   end

Or like this:

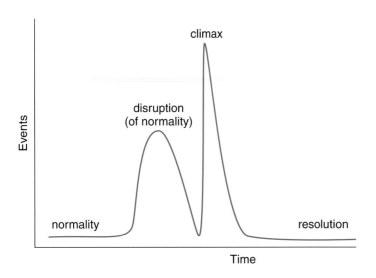

Or even use flashback. This is where the storyteller takes us into the past, as Donovan does in 'A Chitterin Bite'.

Questions

1. How does Donovan create an effective opening (description of normality)?
2. How does she show disruption?
3. What is the climax to the story?
4. How is the story resolved?
5. What is the purpose of the flashback technique?

Characters

There are a number of major, minor (and other) characters in the story.

Task

1. Divide the following into either major or minor characters and state your reasons.
   Try to think whether the story would 'work' without any of the characters.

   Mammy   Alex   Agnes   Mary   Matthew   Jimmy McKeown
   Shuggie   She (Matthew's wife)

Major	Minor	Reason

2. Now complete the chart below by adding **three** traits for each character. This has been started for you.

Character	Trait	Quotation
Mary	1. Uncompromising	'I just broke the last rule'
	2.	
	3.	
Agnes	1.	
	2.	
	3.	
Matthew	1.	
	2.	
	3.	

From setting, plot and character to themes

There is a range of themes in this story. Themes are issues the writer wants us (the readers) to think about and consider.

Task

1. Here is a list of some of the themes in the story. For each one, find evidence to support its inclusion as an issue in this story.

Theme/point	Quotation	Evidence
Choices		
Awkwardness		
Relationships (or their collapse)		
Betrayal		
Friendship		
Childhood and adulthood		
Learning (or not) from experience		

2. Once you have completed the task above, write a mini essay in which you outline the key themes. You can use the TQE (Technique, Quotation, Effect) structure above to help. This has been started for you below:

'A Chitterin Bite', by Anne Donovan, has a range of themes that might be captured under the heading of childhood and adulthood. The story, for example, deals with two stages in the life of Mary: a sequence from her childhood and a sequence from her adulthood. In both cases, what is vital is the nature of her relationships with people of both sexes …

Stage 2: Developing your analysis skills

This requires you to be able to show how the techniques used by Donovan in the story are effective in achieving her writing purpose(s) – the creation of setting, plot, characterisation, structure and themes – although you would not be asked to deal with all of these!

Symbolism

Coldness appears a lot in this story. As such, we can't ignore it. It is there for a reason. There are two forms of cold in this story: literal cold, for example, 'It's freezing cold', and metaphorical or emotional cold where the affair she has is controlled by rules.

Complete the chart below, the first one has been done for you.

Type of cold	Quotation	Effect
Literal	'the shock of the cauld makin us scream as usual'	The memory is recalled powerfully through word choices, 'shock' and 'scream'.
	'a cold draught cut through the heat of the restaurant'	
	'a cauldness grew between us, a damp seepin cauld'	
	'Affairs have their own rules, unspoken'	

Overall effect?

Mary's character, her personality, has changed from the past to the present. Warm and friendly and open as a youngster, she has adopted a cold persona to protect herself from the hurt that can come from relationships. In her childhood, the chitterin bite keeps out physical cold, while, ironically, in adulthood the chitterin bite (the love bite) keeps out emotional cold by subconsciously (or consciously) leading to the end of an affair that is going nowhere.

Language

Scots is used in the childhood sequences while Standard English is used in the adult sequences.

Discuss the effects of the use of different language styles.

Contrast

This is used to compare Mary's childhood to her adulthood. In some cases she retains certain likes from childhood into adulthood; in other cases she does not.

Think about how and where contrast is used throughout the story, and complete the table below.

Quotation	Setting	Effect
	Swimming	
	Clothing	poor child to woman with expensive goods
	Setting	busy, open places to secluded restaurants
	Food	jam sandwiches to expensive Italian meals
	Agnes and Matthew	closeness (Agnes) and distance (Matthew)

Word choice

This, too, is used to help the writer to achieve her purpose(s).

The repetition of the word 'never' at the start of each rule; this is an imperative verb, a command, an instruction. This shows that rigidity of these rules. How can you have such rigid rules for love?

Comment on the effects of the following word choices.

Word choice	Effect
Engraved (p.64)	
Gluthery (p.61)	
Sipping (p.63)	

Flashback, parallel structures or split narrative

As you know, this story is really two stories, each told by alternating between the past and the present. What does the writer gain by using this split narrative technique? What is the effect of the story being told in the first person? 'I still go swimming … I just broke …'

Now that you are an expert on 'A Chitterin Bite', it is time to move on to another story.

'All that Glisters'

From now on, you should read each story, not just individually for what you can 'get out' of it in terms of enjoyment and making you think, but comparatively – in other words, thinking about how it compares with the other stories you have read by Donovan. Remember that these six stories have all been chosen for a reason – there are links between them – perhaps in terms of plot, characters, setting and/or theme. You will spot similarities – and also differences. This makes for exciting reading, keeping us intrigued. It's also something we will return to later, when looking at the final 8-mark question.

Read the story 'All that Glisters' and note down any **three** similarities and **three** differences between this story and 'A Chitterin Bite'. Here are some examples to start you off.

Similarities	Differences
Central character is female	Narrated in Scots
Young	Set in a single time frame
In conflict	Deals with how we deal with death rather than how we deal with life

Plot and narrative

In pairs, rearrange the following sentences into the correct order in which they occur in the story:

- Clare's dad is ill with asbestosis.
- Her aunt won't let her wear bright clothes to the funeral.
- Her teacher gives Clare glitter pens.
- She saves up to buy glitter pens to make the Christmas card.
- She spends time with her dad and talks about 'subtlety'.
- When she gets home, she finds that he has died.
- She covers her dark clothes in glitter.
- The memory of the 'ghosties' game.

Key scenes and how they work

The ghosties game is a recollection Clare has of happier times spent with her father. They clearly get on very well and have a strong relationship. Both child and adult can play and derive mutual pleasure from a simple game. They are secure and comfortable in each other's company. The game epitomises the closeness of their relationship as only they play it and it excludes the other members of the family. At the same time, it represents the father's death as he pretends at this stage to be a ghost while later in the story, he will die for real. This technique is known as **foreshadowing**.

Watch the following:

http://tinyurl.com/lqn2gpp

Choose **either** the scene on subtlety **or** the Christmas card scene and, as above, show how it works.

Narrative mode

This gives you an idea of what happens in the story – the main events. What is equally important is how the story is told. This story is told in the first person. 'I sat … I ran … I jumped.' How does first person narration work? The story is told from the **point of view (POV)** of a single character who also takes part in the plot or action of the story. It is a one-dimensional way of describing thoughts, feelings and observations, but it is also very intense as it describes these reactions at first hand and so everything that happens is shaped through the narrator's own experiences. With this form of storytelling, we are not given access to the point of view of any other characters so we can achieve a deep understanding of the character-narrator.

What are the advantages and disadvantages of first person narration? Write down the headings 'advantages' and 'disadvantages' in your workbook and decide which of the following statements belong under which heading. Copy them into your workbook.

- Intense
- Builds bond between reader and character
- No other POV considered
- One-dimensional
- Creates empathy/sympathy with audience
- Deep understanding of character
- Personal tone
- 'Connection' to character
- Thoughts and feelings are rendered directly
- Without being diluted by other POV
- Reader 'hears' the voice of the character directly

As you can see, this way of telling a story helps to create the character of Clare; it is part of her characterisation. What else helps to build this characterisation?

Realism and Scots

The use of the Glaswegian dialect helps to locate the story, to place it geographically, and to place it in our minds. Scottish readers, in particular, might recognise the familiar speech patterns and may 'connect' to those patterns. This makes the events and the characters all the more real. As such, we believe in them. We sympathise with them. We care about what happens to them. This carries us deep into the story and makes us want to read to the end. The added benefit of using Scots is that the characters appear to have a charm, honesty and sincerity. As such, we warm to them.

Setting

The setting in time is in present day Glasgow, although it looks back to a past event – the death of Clare's dad. In terms of place, it has two settings: school and home, both of which would be recognisable to Scottish readers.

Find **two** pieces of evidence to justify the above.

Characterisation

The name 'Clare' means 'bright' or 'clear'. The Spanish word for 'clear', for example, is 'claro'. Why is Clare an apt name for this character?

Select **five** of the words below that describe Clare. Find evidence from the story to support your choices.

selfish	positive	irritating	mature	intelligent	loyal	respectful	colourful
charming	straightforward	observant	shy	determined	artistic	honest	caring
loving	cheeky	odd	deceitful	anxious	arrogant		

Sample answer

In the words, '… even though ah can see the sense in whit Jimmy's sayin, well, ma daddy says stealin is stealin, and ah canny go against his word,' Clare clearly proves her honesty, loyalty, maturity and determination. By far the easiest option open to Clare is to steal the pens, but her respect and love for her dad compels her not to.

Relationship with Clare's dad

Find evidence of Clare's close relationship with her father.

Look closely at what she does (plot), and what she says (dialogue), to reveal her thoughts, feelings and reactions.

Hint!

Try these areas of the story:

- Spending time with her dad and the 'subtle' use of glitter
- The way in which she gets the pens
- Her childhood memories
- The effort she puts into the making of the card
- What she does on the day of the funeral.

Relationship with Aunt Pauline – technique

Questions

When Aunt Pauline sees Clare's outfit, '… her face froze over …'

1. What techniques are being used here?
2. What are their effects?
3. What do you, as a reader, feel about Aunt Pauline?

Relationship with Clare's dad – technique

Questions

When Clare learns of her dad's death the '… shouts were muffled as if in a fog …'

1. What techniques are being used?
2. What are their effects?
3. How do they show her emotional reaction to the news?

Dissociation

This is a technique used to show the process of a character disconnecting from a traumatic situation. In this story, the author shows how death can impact on people in very different ways. Below is an example of this technique in action:

'Blue veins criss-crossed the back of her haun. Why were veins blue when blood wis red?'

If you were asked to show how this technique works, by referring to this text, you could say:

Dissociation is a technique used to help us at traumatic moments in our lives. It helps us to process the trauma. It cushions the blow. In this case, Clare is diverted from the horror of her dad's death because of her preoccupation with people's hands and with the fact that red blood appears to be blue. Because she is not thinking about her dad's death, she is not feeling any pain.

Your turn

Show how this technique works through close reference to the line below.

'… the coldness shot through me till ah felt ma bones shiverin and ah heard a voice …'

Symbolism

For each of the following quotes, consider what effects are created.

Glitter/colour

'… the glitter jist brought everythin tae life, gleamin and glistenin agin the flat cardboard …'

Asbestos/dark

'… breathin in stour aw day …'

Hands

Hands can represent many positive things: closeness, a connection with other people, friendship. They can also represent negative things: anger, threat, violence.

Stains

Stains are used to suggest the father's illness and the fact that it will never go away; it is terminal.

Find a quotation to show the use of stains in this way.
Then build up the 'Technique Quotation Explanation/Effect' (TQE) structure around it. You are starting with the 'T'.

Imagery

This is all about the pictures the writer deliberately tries to create in our minds. If, for example, you think about the word 'enormous' it creates a particular picture in the mind.

Write down **three** things that spring to mind when you read the word 'enormous'.

The key idea, the defining part of the image concerns size. The word describes not only something big, but towards the biggest end of the big scale. It's really BIG. It's HUGE. Maybe even bigger than HUGE.

> **Connotative meaning** is the very particular meanings or ideas associated with a word.

1. Place these words along the arrow in order of intensity:

   dislike   hate   despise   detest   abhor

   ———————————————————►

   intensity

Colour imagery is used very particularly in this story: light versus dark; bright versus dim; glitter versus dust/asbestos. The red coat and rainbow-coloured glitter represents positivity, life, endurance.

2. Find **two** examples of dark and light imagery. Comment on their functions.
3. Which of these could be a theme in the story and why?

   death   loss   hate   jealousy   love   family   violence   revenge   old age

   parent–child relationships   coping with trauma

Title

The title is a reference to the Shakespeare play *The Merchant of Venice*, the full line being, 'All that glisters is not gold'. 'Glisters' is also an unusual word, meaning 'glitters'. The meaning is that, just because something appears to be good, it doesn't mean that it is good. This makes the title something of a puzzle for the reader as we try to connect it to the plot.

In groups, discuss how the title of the story links to its content.

Choose a novel or a short story with a message in its title that is still relevant today.

Mini model answer

'All that Glisters', by Anne Donovan, is a short story that deals with an issue that will always be relevant – death.

> Story/Text. Author. Link to question

Donovan explores the theme of death through the use of a range of techniques, which will be explored through the amplification of two key scenes, the first of which is the debate between Clare and her dad on the idea of subtlety.

This scene has a number of functions. It depicts the closeness of this adult–child relationship and highlights its depth (as they can talk about anything) in order to make us realise more profoundly the impact on Clare when her dad dies at the end.

'What did she mean, subtle, hen? How wis it subtle?

… Ah took his haun in mines and turnt it roon so his palm faced upward … the imprint of ma finger left sparkly wee trails a light …

… Aye, hen, Subtle.'

> Quotation

This scene serves a number of functions.

> Point

It foreshadows (prepares) us for the final scene in which Clare dresses in bright colours and glitter as she believes (rightly) that it would please her dad.

> Technique

It also uses irony to make a thematic point that glitter is not usually described as subtle, but its use here could be described as 'subtle' as she is really trying to cheer up her dad. Another interpretation is that she is playing the part of teacher by showing and not telling as the blotting of the glitter makes it more 'subtle'. In this way a picture is built up of the intimacy of their relationship.

> Technique

> Evidence. Analysis

As this close connection is heightened, we realise the devastating impact the death will have on Clare at the close of the story and so we sympathise with her deeply as her father's death will plainly impact on her strongly.

> Link to question. Evaluation

Task

Now write your own response for a second key scene.

'Away in a Manger'

Again, we have a young, female central character. Again, the setting is Glasgow. This time, the setting in time is very specific – the centre of Glasgow just prior to Christmas. A new theme is added to the mix, though, as we deal with the problem of homelessness and its morality. More widely, there is the idea that to some problems, there are no easy solutions.

Title

Listen to the lyrics of the carol here:

http://tinyurl.com/pszl4aw

What are the links between the carol and the story? Here's something to get you started.

Carol
Celebrates the birth of Christ

Story
Christmas setting

Plot summary

Amy and her mother go to see the Christmas lights at George Square. The place is busy with late night shoppers. They look at the nativity scene and see a poor man sleeping. He then wakes up and Amy thinks that he is an angel, but realises later that he is just an ordinary man. Afterwards, they go on the bus back to their safe home separated from the harsh reality of Glasgow life.

Key incidents

1. Visit to George Square
2. Observing a poor man sleeping at a nativity scene
3. Return back to their safe home away the centre of the city

Narrative mode

Third-person interior monologue is where the central character relates his/her own thoughts and feelings as if s/he is hearing them inside his/her own head. In this way, the thoughts passing through the minds of the characters are revealed to the reader. This allows the author to convey not only thoughts, but also impressions, feelings and reactions. Normally, we don't get to hear what is going on inside someone's head – to discover what they're really thinking. This means that we see everything from the POV of the narrator and so we feel close to them.

Sandra and Amy

Characterisation

Sandra

Which words 'characterise' her? Find evidence from the text to justify your answer.

loud   sensible   easy-going   harassed   interesting   immature   disrespectful
independent   unhelpful   kind   selfish   confident   honest   strict   hard-working
bad-tempered   observant   cold   determined   brave

Amy

Which words 'characterise' her? Find evidence from the text to justify your answer.

brave   bad-mannered   loving   unselfish   dishonest   happy   immature   artistic
cheeky   thoughtful   polite   confident   naive   talkative   determined   silly   curious
disrespectful   independent

Sandra and Amy are close. We know this from what they do (actions/plot), from what they say (dialogue), and from what they think as we are given access to their thoughts and feelings by the interior monologue. Find evidence to support the idea that they are close.

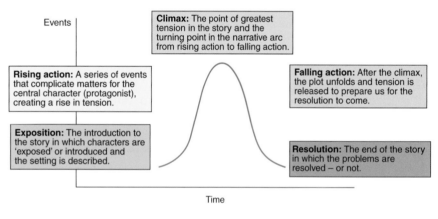

Identify **one** part of the story for each of the above headings.

Scottish text analysis

As we noted in the Introduction, this forms part of your National 5 English examination, in which you are asked to read an extract from a text you have previously studied and then attempt to answer questions on it. It is worth 20 marks and you are advised to spend 45 minutes on it in the critical reading paper.

This activity examines your ability to analyse part of a text and then relate this to the remainder of the text and, thereafter, to another text or texts by the same author. Let's start slowly, though. Read the passage below and attempt the questions that follow.

Huddled in the straw, hidden in a corner behind the figure of a large beast, lay a man. He was slightly built, dressed in auld jeans and a thin jaicket. One of his feet stuck oot round the end of the statue and on it was a worn trainin shoe, the cheapest kind they sold in the store. Sandra moved round tae get a better look at him. He was quite young, wi a pointed face and longish dark hair. A stubbly growth covered his chin. He seemed sound asleep.

'Is he an angel, Mammy?'

Sandra didn't answer. She wis lookin at the glass structure wonderin how on earth he'd got in. One of the panels at the back looked bit loose, but you'd think they'd have an alarm on it. Lucky for him they never – at least he'd be warm in there. She was that intent on the glass panels that she'd nearly forgotten he wisnae a statue. Suddenly he opened his eyes. They were grey.

Amy grabbed her mother's arm and started jumpin up and down.

'Mammy, look, he's alive! Look Mammy. He's an angel!'

'Naw, he's no an angel. He's a man.'

'But Mammy, whit's he daein in there wi the baby Jesus?'

'Ah don't know. Mibbe he's naewhere tae stay.'

'How no, Mammy?'

'Ah don't know, Amy. Some folk don't have anywhere to stay.'

Questions

1. What are the main events in this scene? **(2 marks)**
2. What techniques does the writer use to gain our sympathy for the man? **(4 marks)**
3. How does the writer emphasise the difference between Amy's reaction and her mother's to the sight of the man? **(2 marks)**

Possible answers

1. Before

Any two

Setting is just before Christmas ... Amy and her mum are in Glasgow to see the Christmas lights ... Sandra sees this time of the year in terms of extra work as she works in a shop.

After

Any two

Sandra refuses to house the homeless man ... She gives excuses for not taking him in ... Sandra threatens Amy with no presents this year ... They return home.

2. Techniques

Word choices:

Position

'Huddled' tight, foetal position as a defence against the cold. Reminds us of a baby/Jesus.

'Hidden' hiding from the gaze of onlookers or not seen by the onlookers, who are so distracted by the images that they can't see the reality.

Supporting detail

'In the straw' out of the way. Trying to stay warm. Like Jesus.

'In a corner' out of sight. Away from people.

'Behind the figure of a large beast' hidden. Out of sight. Avoiding contact with people. Reminds us of the nativity scene with the man taking the place of Jesus.

Dress

'Slightly built' – thin/undernourished

'Auld jeans' – poor

'Thin jaicket' – poor/susceptible to cold

'Worn trainin shoe' – not good enough for Glasgow winter. Poor

'The cheapest kind they sold in the store' – very poor.

Appearance

Young ... thin ... angular features ... beard ... long hair ... reminds us of Jesus.

3. Amy – very interested, as suggested by range of questions: 'Who's that Mammy?' ... 'Is he an angel, Mammy?' ... Naivety ... Innocence ... Excited ... 'Amy grabbed her mother's arm and started jumpin up and down.' ... Exclamation marks – high excitement ... Actions – excitement is barely contained ... Continued questioning – trying to make sense of an adult/confusing world.

'Dear Santa'

Setting

The setting of the story is, again, Glasgow at Christmas, where the action alternates between Alison at home and her meeting with 'Santa' in Debenham's store in the centre of Glasgow. This setting creates sympathy for Alison as the events happen at a time that is supposed to be about joy and happiness and, during this time, Alison is very unhappy.

Task

1. Write a brief summary of the plot.
2. Decide which character these quotes refer to and then read the notes on characterisation.

Character	Quotation	Effect
	'fair curly hair'	angelic appearance/feminine
	'big lurkin thing'	ungainly/large

Characterisation

Alison's character is likeable and we find that we are 'on her side'. She is at a stage where she is growing up and leaving childhood behind. This makes her very aware of her surroundings and, at the same time, her attention to nuances, or subtleties, is very advanced for her years. This device allows Alison's feelings to be described to the reader in great detail, which makes her hurt feelings all the more poignant. The writer then contrasts Alison with her younger sister to show why Alison felt jealous and unloved.

Task

Key incidents

Write about the purposes of the **four** key incidents in the story. Each one has been started for you.

Incident 1

Alison's comparison to her sister, Katie, in the play. The connotations of a shepherd and an angel. How do these represent their characters? Alison is seen as a babysitter …

Incident 2

The 'plastercine' incident – shows Alison's jealousy towards her sister. After putting the 'plastercine' on her sister's face Alison feels 'good inside, warm and full' …

Incident 3

Her belief in Santa changes, 'I don't think I believe in Santa any mair but don't want tae admit it.' This shows that although she doesn't believe in Santa she still has hope because she doesn't want to give up on it. This is in comparison to what she feels for her mother …

Incident 4

The end of the story when her mum tucks her into bed – 'She goes oot, nearly closing the door, but leaving a wee crack of light fallin across the bedclothes.' This shows …

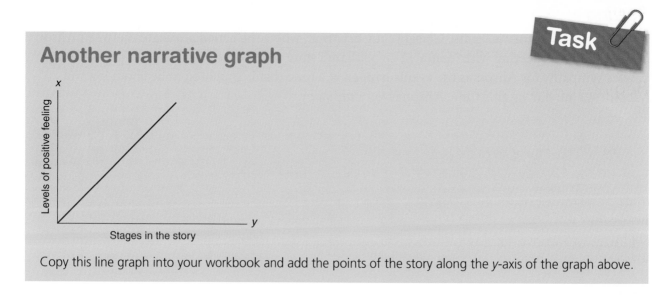

Another narrative graph

Copy this line graph into your workbook and add the points of the story along the *y*-axis of the graph above.

Language

The language is simple as it has to convince the reader that a child is really telling the story. Despite its simplicity, it provides the reader with clear images that let us into Alison's state of mind, such as 'heavy and grey lik a stane'. The fact that the story is written in Scots helps us to believe that these events could have happened and also allows us to identify with the central character because we, too, may have experienced these feelings at one point as they are very common.

Here are some quotations from the story. Where do they come from in the story and what are the effects of the word choices?

Quotation	Location	Effect
'It's hard no tae be seen, it makes you wee and crumpled up inside.'		
'Her skin creases, soft and squashy like a marshmallow.'		
'ah'm this big lurkin thing at the endy the back row, daurk and blurred'		
'… watchin her hair glowin like a halo against the blackness of the room'		
'… a dry kiss, barely grazin ma cheek …'		
'… She goes oot, nearly closin the door, but leavin a wee crack of light fallin across the bedclothes'		

Narrative mode

The story is written in the **first person narrative** from the perspective of Alison. This helps to engage the reader by giving them an insight into the thoughts and feelings of the girl. The story is written in Scots to give a sense of realism and to make it more believable. In addition to this, the use of this specific narrative mode makes the reader sympathetic to the girl telling the story. The reader is involved in the story as this girl talks about the worries and doubts in her life. The use of the present tense takes away the benefit of hindsight. This makes the girl's troubles seem worse than they really are because they are happening now – in the heat of the moment.

Beginning and ending

The title, 'Dear Santa', immediately captures the reader's attention and hooks the reader into wanting to know more. What kind of letter to Santa will this be? What will the wee girl wish for? This is followed up by the opening line, 'Ma mammy disnae love me', which surprises and shocks the reader, at which point we must read on to find out why the speaker feels as she does.

The ending of the story contrasts with its opening in that her mother gives Alison hope that she loves her, saying, 'There's nothing wrang wi' broon hair'. Symbolically, the mother leaves the door open slightly at the end letting 'a wee crack of light' fall across Alison's bed, which suggests that there is always hope and that things will work out just fine between Alison and her mother in the end.

Textual temperature – tone

Words have emotional charges or temperatures. They can be positive or negative, good or bad, nice or nasty, or they can make you hot or cold about someone or something. When a writer uses words like the ones above, s/he wants to position you, the reader, in a certain way, to make you sympathetic or unsympathetic to a particular character.

Students often have difficulty with questions on tone.

Task

1. Copy the line below into your workbook and place the following words on the line according to their charges.

Positive	Neutral	Negative

dislike   anger   hateful   despise   love   like   adore   worship

2. What emotion are you supposed to feel when you read the following words? How are you meant to react? (You might need to use a dictionary!)

glutton   evil   lascivious   bloated   abhorrent   acerbic   vile

3. How charged is the opening line of 'Dear Santa'? How are we meant to feel for the character?

Themes

This short story shows that the world through the eyes of a child is not as innocent as one may think. It also deals with pressing issues that many children face today such as jealousy, child neglect and the need for attention.

Jealousy	Alison's jealousy of her sister: 'In the photy she's at the front, in between Mary and Joseph, glittern as if she really wis an angel, an ahm this big lurkin thing at the endy the back row, daurk and blurred.'
Realisation	Alison is growing up: 'And Alison getting awful big fur her age. Ah know, ah kin hardly get anything tae fit her.' This is also seen when Santa says 'You are a big girl for eight, aren't you?'
Favouritism	We see that Alison believes that Katie is favoured over her: 'Ma daddy says she's a princess, her teacher says she's an angel, ma mammy says *Why can't you be more like your sister?*' Also 'Gonnae come and tuck me in, mammy?' 'You're too big to be tucked in.'
Love	The love between the family, between mother and daughter: 'My mammy disnae love me. A kin see it in her eyes.'
Hope	The light shining on the bed shows that Alison has hope that her mum does love her 'She goes oot, nearly closing the door, but leaving a wee crack of light fallin across the bedclothes.'

Questions

Read lines 1–30 from 'Ma mammy …' to '… more like your sister' and answer the questions below.

1. What is Alison's main problem in this extract and what evidence is there to support your answer? **(2 marks)**
2. What techniques are used in lines 1–8 to emphasise Alison's feelings? **(4 marks)**
3. In lines 9–15 Donovan adds evidence to support Alison's view that her mother prefers her sister, Katie. What kind of evidence? **(2 marks)**
4. Read lines 16–22. Alison thinks back to a time before, when her sister was very young. How do we know she was jealous even then? **(2 marks)**
5. This story deals with troubled relationships. Identify how this theme is explored in this and at least one other story by Donovan. **(8 marks)**

Possible answers

1. Thinks she is unloved by her mum/jealous of little sister/feels isolated/can't compete with younger sister.

   (She is unhappy will gain 0 marks.)

   Any one

   The way her Mum looks at her/Mum doesn't return her kisses/tells her what to do (TV off in ten minutes)/won't tuck her in/tucks Katie in/ignores her by continuing to watch TV/thinks her Mum used to love her before Katie was born/uses 'plastercine' to cover Katie's face/thinks Katie looks perfect/Dad and teacher also think Katie's perfect/feels Mum wants her to be more like younger sister.

   Any two

2. Take things line by line:

The short, blunt opening statement 'hook' is shocking after the title. This is followed by a longer explanation of her reasons for claiming this.

She can see it in her eyes. Looks through Alison; not at her. Mother has become used to Alison, who feels she's being treated like a household object.

Her reaction to this treatment is then given. She feels that it is hard on her. Literally, it makes her feel small and it is painful, 'crumpled up inside'. Metaphorically, it makes her seem less significant than her sister, less important, something that can be 'crumpled up' as if for disposal.

Alison is conscious of her mother's age and that she does not react physically. She accepts the kiss, but it seems to bring no pleasure.

Mother does not return kisses. Blunt statement/short sentences for impact. First person present for immediacy. Glasgow dialect for realism/identification with character/sympathy. Word choices, 'wee ... crumpled ... skin creases ... squashy'. Simile. Skin is like a marshmallow. Soft. Pliable. Very white. Pallid.

Any two

3. Limited reading time then an instruction, 'Light's tae be aff.'

Refusal to tuck her in, 'Too big.'

Mother ignores her and 'Keeps watchin the television.'

Contrasting Alison with Katie, 'Katie's only five; you're a big girl.'

The reality of Alison's age is brought out. She's only eight herself.

4. A key incident is related to justify Alison's point. Alison's reaction to her mother's attitude leads to her projecting her feelings onto her little sister. This is symbolised in the attempt to make Katie out to be the opposite of what she is – ugly. This makes Alison feel better.

5. **Commonality**

This is a general understanding of whatever the 'link' between the extract and the wider work, e.g. understanding of how Donovan develops the theme of troubled relationships in her stories. Up to 2 marks can be achieved for identifying elements of **commonality** as identified in the question. A further 2 marks can be achieved for **reference to the extract given**. An additional 4 marks can be awarded for similar references to **at least one other text/part of the text** by the writer. Perhaps the easiest way to deal with this question is like this:

(i) Deal with the theme as it emerges in the extract. **(2 marks)**
(ii) Deal with the theme as it emerges in **one** or more other stories by Donovan.
     The commonality bit. **(2 marks)**
(iii) Deal with similar references. **(4 marks)**

- The theme is troubled relationships between a child and adults.
- In this case, it's between a daughter, her younger sister, and the mother.
- Alison believes she is the victim of favouritism.
- She gives evidence to support this, such as her mum's refusal to tuck her in bed at night, the way she stares through her, and the way in which she does not return her kisses.
- The 'plastercine' scene emphasises this as Alison's reaction is to take it out on her younger sister.
- The 'Santa' scene emphasises the difficult relationship between mother and daughter as even another adult, Santa, comments openly and hurtfully about her size for her age.
- The 'letter' scene, however, brings the story to a positive conclusion as Alison and her mother share a moment of tenderness.
- Use of first person narrative to allow direct access to Alison's feelings thus emphasising the theme of her isolation.
- Use of dialect so that we 'connect' with Alison and therefore empathise with her. We will also be aware of this 'common' theme in families and may even have experienced it first-hand.

→

Another text

This is about connecting the key part of the question to at least one other story by the same author. There are 4 marks available for this.

- Second story is 'Away in a Manger', which shares the theme of troubled relationships between mother and daughter. This is shown in the breakdown in communication between the central character and her mother through the central theme of homelessness.
- The daughter takes a child-like, naive, humane approach to the homeless man. She wants to bring him home. The mother's view is that of an adult who dismisses the idea without a second thought.
- There is also a sense of maternal preoccupation in this story as the mother is in a hurry to see the Christmas lights and to return home as soon as possible.
- The disconnection between adult and child is seen through the dialogue as the young girl continually asks questions to show her difficulty in coming to terms with the adult world, while the mother attempts to divert her daughter.
- Ultimately, the messages are morally ambiguous. Who is right in 'Away in a Manger'? Mother or daughter? Equally, who is right in 'Dear Santa'? Isn't the real truth that there are favourites in every family and that it is just part of life?

Hint!
Think about key events.

'Virtual Pals'

Setting

In time, the story is set in 2001. Remember that this is well before Facebook and Twitter. Fewer people had access to the internet at home and schools didn't have as many computers as they now do. It has two settings in place: Glasgow and Jupiter. Both settings are connected by the emails between Siobhan and Irina through which the story is told.

Task

Write a brief summary of the plot.

Key incidents

1. Irina's first email reply suggests that the email communication has gone further than was intended and establishes the cultural differences between the two characters.
2. Siobhan's revelation about having feelings towards a boy shows how difficult being a teenager can be.
3. Irina's response to this email shows the different backgrounds and cultures.
4. Siobhan's termination of the emails shows her changeability and leaves us with a cliffhanger. Will the emails return?

Characterisation

Decide which of these words and phrases apply to Siobhan and which apply to Irina and place them under the relevant column. Then find a quotation to support your decision.

confident   easily embarrassed   free spirited   child-like   thoughtful   under-confident

unhappy   humorous   cheeky   bossy   serious   friendly   honest   intelligent

dishonest   loving   practical   sticks to her beliefs   unintelligent   observant

easily led   determined   shy   immature

Siobhan	Irina	Quotation

Purpose

In 'Virtual Pals', Anne Donovan illustrates the confusion and emotional turmoil of adolescence and maturation whilst exploring Glaswegian/Scots mannerisms and dialect in comparison with Standard English.

Themes

Read the notes in the chart below and then find an event to show where this theme emerges in the story.

Theme	Event
Gender: Both characters have different ways of looking at boys and relationships so they have different ideas about gender roles. Irina comes from a society where men and women are equal; Siobhan does not. Siobhan finds Irina's world confusing and Irina finds Siobhan's world confusing, too.	
Social differences and education: The characters are the same age, but they come from very different backgrounds. This is shown in their language and in their lives. Siobhan's parents have working class retail/trade jobs while Irina's parents have middle class/scientific jobs. Their educational backgrounds seem very different, too. Whilst Irina's formal tone of email seems artificial, we warm to Siobhan's informal language.	
Digital communication: Through a communication error an email to a school in Shetland arrives at a school on Jupiter and shows us that digital communication can break all boundaries. This device is used by the author to allow us to look at our familiar world through unfamiliar eyes so that we can see it differently.	
Adolescence: Siobhan is approaching 13 years old and is facing the difficult time of puberty. She is aware of boys, confused about her feelings towards one and also shows signs of mood changes. Irina is also going through adolescence, but her reaction to it is very different. Irina's scientific understanding of sex means that she considers Siobhan's feelings to be 'unhealthy' because, in her society, both men and women are equal.	

Language

Discuss. Both characters speak in the way that is appropriate on their respective planets. What message is being communicated by the author?

Question

Write a mini essay of 500 words on the following question:

Short stories often concern current issues. Choose one such story and then go on to describe briefly the issues and the techniques used to highlight the key theme.

'Zimmerobics'

Plot summary

Task

Complete this plot summary:

The story begins with the old lady describing the sheltered _____, revealing her reluctance to be there. The speaker is pressured by her niece, _____, to get more involved. At first, she is _____, but this changes when she meets _____, a fitness instructor who is beginning a _____ called _____. The speaker does join the class and _____ it and she begins to _____ with the other members of the class. Their class is to be _____ for promotional purposes and the story ends with the class watching themselves on the _____ .

Characterisation

Task

1. Complete the grid below by finding evidence that Miss Knight is portrayed sympathetically, while Catherine is portrayed unsympathetically.

Miss Knight – sympathetic	Catherine – unsympathetic
Aches and pains	Doesn't really listen to her aunt
Attempts to tell niece of her feelings	Hurries to get away
Doesn't always say what she is thinking	Speaks in short sentences

2. Which of these words could be used to describe Miss Knight at the start of the story?

gloomy   dreamy   observant   determined   lonely   good humoured   depressed

unemotional   shy   immobile   snobbish   funny   unsociable   selfish

3. Now create your own word bank to describe her at the end of the story. This has been started for you:

sociable   cheerful   mobile   …

Key incidents

1. Interaction with daughter.
2. Miss Knight tries the exercise class, enjoys it and returns.
3. Miss Knight is given a tracksuit so that she looks the part at the class and takes part in an exercise video filming.

Language/voice

Task

This story is told in English or in a Scottish form of Standard English in the first person so we can see into Miss Knight's thoughts and views on things. Discuss what this tells us about the character of Miss Knight.

Purpose

This is a first person narrative from the perspective of an old lady recently moved into a sheltered house. The perspective gives an insight into how the woman would have felt at this difficult transition in her life. It shows her reluctance to accept her new life and how an exercise class changes that.

Themes

- Old age
- Family
- Friendship
- New experiences
- Parent–child relationships

Techniques

Here are a number of techniques that are used in the story together with quotations. Describe their effects.

Technique	Quotation	Effect(s)
Onomatopoeia	'zim, zim, zim'/'clicking and crunking'	Mirrors movement and sound of zimmer
Simile	'like the central-heating boiler starting up'	
Metaphor	'my nerves and my blood coming alive inside me'	
Personification	'soft, fleecy material that stroked my skin as I moved'	
Capitalisation	'MEET'	
Short sentences	'I do.'	
Rhetorical questions	'I don't care so why should she?'	
Use of Scots	'humphy-backit'	
Comparison	'It was like starting school and discovering that the others were wearing school uniform and you weren't.'	

Ending

Read the start of the story and its ending. Discuss what has changed.

Question

Write a mini essay of 500 words on the following question:

Some short stories deal with conflict. Choose one such story and then go on to describe briefly the nature of the conflict and the techniques used to highlight the key themes of the story.

Finally ...

Overarching connections between the stories

Characterisation	• Many characters in the stories have an element of **awkwardness**. In 'All that Glisters' the girl wants to go to the funeral in a red outfit because her father liked it. • In 'A Chitterin Bite' the character does not agree with her friend's wishes as a child and, as an adult, she breaks the rules of cheating by giving her lover a love bite. Thus, she too is rebellious. • 'Away in a Manger' sees an innocent child begging to take a stranger home. • In 'Zimmerobics', Miss Knight is a character who will also not do as she is told. • In 'Virtual Pals' social awkwardness in Siobhan is seen. • The main character in 'Dear Santa' feels that her mother does not love her. A very awkward situation for a young girl.
Innocence and truth	• Prominent in both 'Away in a Manger' and 'A Chitterin Bite'. In the latter story the young woman, as a girl, loses her innocent sense of friendship when her friend pairs her up with her date's pal. In the former story, the mother tries to maintain the innocence of the child and focus her on the modern Christmas message, to do with gifts and bright lights, while diverting her away from the more serious part of it, which is to do with sharing what you have with strangers. • Innocence is important in Donovan's work. Her narrators are often girls who have not left childhood and innocence behind. In 'Dear Santa', for example, the main character admits she knows Santa does not exist but she wants to believe in him.
Point of view and imagery	• In 'Away in a Manger', the main event is the mother taking the girl to see the Christmas lights in Glasgow. The child wants to look at the lights, but the mother sees and is aware of the others – the homeless. • In 'Zimmerobics' the narrator is tired of looking at things and so she can't bring herself to watch the film. The exercise class seems to revive the sense of colour: 'The track suit was emerald green'. • In 'All that Glisters', visual effects are central to the plot. • In 'A Chitterin Bite' the bite mark on the man's shoulder blade, in a place where he will not see it but where his wife will. She waits, unseen, outside Bellini's café for her friend.
Female characters	• Her characters are mainly female and her main characters in these stories are all female. • They are awkward, yet independent.
English and Scots	• The narrators use Scots. • It is realistic to use this as it is the language of the people of Scotland. • It tells the stories of ordinary people from their point of view. • It shows the value of Scots as a language in its own right. • When English is used, it is seen to be less than effective in conveying genuine feeling.
Language as a character	• In 'A Chitterin Bite', the main character shifts between Scots and English as she alternates between childhood and adulthood. • In 'Virtual Pals' the alternate use of Scots and English defines the two characters. The character who uses Scots has difficulty growing up. Irina's use of English suggests that she is completely in control of herself.

Mental map

You can create your own mental map using the software at the website below. This will help to show the interrelationships between the stories. It is better if you do this personally as there is more chance that it will then 'stick' in your mind as an examination aid. Use this mental map to join together the overarching connections described above.

www.examtime.com

PART ONE

CHAPTER 2
EDWIN MORGAN

Homework

One of the skills that will be demanded of you on the course is the ability to work independently. To help you with this, try the activity below.

Write an infographic about Edwin Morgan. It should be a piece of biographical research using the resources below. The main purpose is to give key information about the man and his poetry in a graphic form.

Online resources

- http://tinyurl.com/pf3zeon, from the BBC, provides a useful survey of Morgan's works.
- www.edwinmorgan.com has a helpful biography for students.
- Edwin Morgan Archive at the Scottish Poetry Library (edwinmorgan.scottishpoetrylibrary.org.uk) contains a timeline of his life.
- http://tinyurl.com/l3eedb, also from the BBC, contains a useful audio feature allowing you to listen to the material.

Once you have completed the homework, narrow your blurb down to **three** key facts about Morgan. Share these with your partner.

Texts

There are six poems in this collection. Morgan's poems here deal with people, places and animals. On first inspection, these might appear to be quite different, but when we look closer, we see the interconnections.

People

'**In the Snack-bar**' deals with the isolation of disabled people. To highlight this, Morgan describes an old man struggling to find his way to the toilet in a café in Glasgow.

'**Good Friday**' deals with alcoholism and religion. The poet achieves this by describing the reflections of a man on a bus. The setting for this poem, like '**In the Snack-bar**', is Glasgow.

'**Trio**' is also set in Glasgow. It, too, deals with religion, but it is more positive in its outlook than the other two poems as it also deals with another aspect of Glasgow life – friendship.

Places

'**Winter**' is the first of the poems to deal with a place. It is also set in Glasgow and it deals with the idea of things changing. Like the others, it has a very recognisable setting within Glasgow – Bingham's pond near Great Western Road at the back of the Pond hotel.

'**Slate**' is very different from the others in terms of its setting in time and place. Like '**Winter**', it deals with the theme of change and nature. This setting is no longer Glasgow, but the actual creation of another part of Scotland – the Isle of Lewis.

Animals

'**Hyena**' is the only poem in the collection to deal with an animal – a hyena. When we think of these creatures, we think of hateful scavengers, but Morgan sees value even in a hyena and forces us to see it differently. The themes are: death, life and survival. The setting for the poem is now very far from Glasgow – Africa.

'In the Snack-bar'

Textual explosion!

This way of adding notes to a text helps you to figure out how it works.

Read the opening section of the poem and the comment boxes below.

'In the Snack-bar'

Alliteration on the letter 'c' amplifies the sound and the onomatopoeia on 'clatter' conveys the idea of an annoying, resonating, high-pitched sound.

'Clatter' is onomatopoeic. High pitched. Irritating. Would draw attention.

A cup capsizes along the formica,

slithering with a dull clatter.

A few heads turn in the crowded evening snack-bar.

An old man is trying to get to his feet

from the low round stool fixed to the floor.

The onomatopoeic 'slithering' suggests the cup's snake-like movement along the bar and the present participle slows the action.

Use of the indefinite form 'An' suggests the narrator has no relationship with him.

Present participle slows down time and examines the process of him trying to get up. It is happening very slowly.

In lines 1–3 we have the explanation for the fallen cup. Dropped by an old man who is struggling to regain his footing.

Despite the clamour, no real attention is drawn. 'A few' suggests some people do notice it even in the 'crowded evening' snack-bar. The old man is isolated.

Task

In pairs, fill in the blanks below using the TQE technique for lines 7–11.
Line 6 has already been done for you.

Technique (T)	Quotation (Q)	Effect (E)
Line 6 Thematic variation	'slowly'	Stretching out the action by placing the word 'slowly' at the start of the sentence
Line 7 Transferred epithet	'Dismal hump'	
Line 8 Present participle		Slows down time
Line 9	'stands … stained'	Sounds like sigh
Line 10 Simile		
Line 11 Alliteration	'sways slightly'	

Textual explosion!

Lines 12–21 are have been deconstructed for you below.

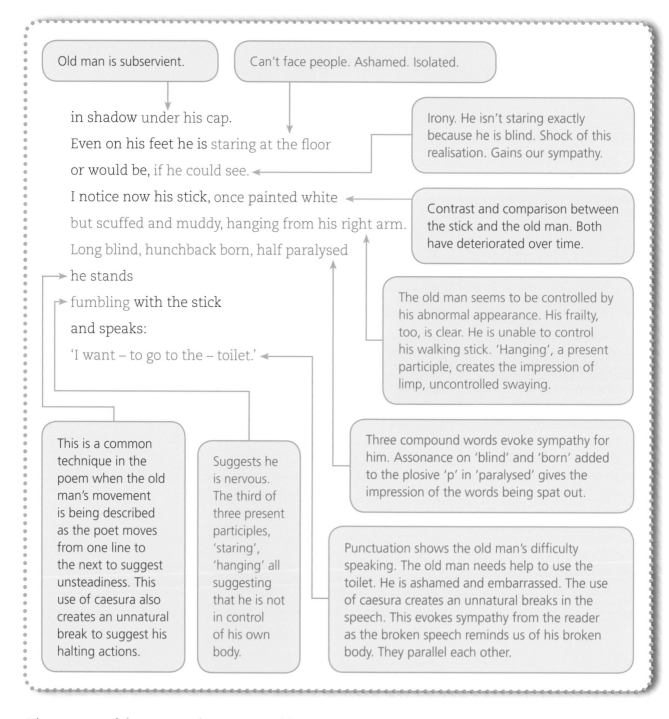

This section of the poem in lines 12–21 adds to the pathos of the old man as we discover that not only is he hunchbacked, he is also blind and 'half paralysed'. We are allowed to observe the events in the café, as the narrator responds to the man's request to go to the toilet. The narrator plays two parts in the poem: he tells the 'story' of the poem and he also takes part in that story.

What next?

The next section describes their journey to the toilet. It reminds us of the stranger who helped Jesus to carry his cross on the road to Calvary. Here, the journey is downwards, though, as if descending into hell rather than ascending into heaven.

The narrator finds it difficult to communicate with the old man who is unable to communicate fluently. They both make it to the toilet. Here, the narrator waits for the man. It is clear that the man depends completely on other people to do even the most basic of things.

Task

Google search 'Calvary'. What effect is Morgan trying to achieve by using this reference?

At the end of the poem, the narrator helps the old man onto a bus where the conductor also struggles to communicate with the old man. This means that his disability makes it difficult for both him and others. It is a problem with a double edge.

The final part of the poem returns to the thoughts of the narrator, who reflects on the meeting and, in doing so, engages the reader.

Finally

What would you have done in the narrator's situation?

Questions

Read lines 1–24 of the poem again and answer the questions below.

Try to answer questions 1–3 in pairs.

1. Identify the main theme and give a reason to show how you know this. **(2 marks)**
2. Show how any two examples of the poet's language highlight this theme. **(4 marks)**
3. What is the effect of each of the words 'staring', 'hanging' and 'fumbling'? **(3 marks)**

In this part of the examination paper you will also be asked a final question which can be tackled as a series of short answers; it does **not** have to be a mini essay. We will look in more detail at this type of question later. Right now, just read the question below.

4. By referring closely to this text and at least one other poem by Morgan, show how he creates characters with whom we sympathise. **(8 marks)**

Possible answers

Markers' meeting

Once you have completed the questions, skim read the answer key below. Then swap jotters with your partner. Each of you should apply the answer key to your partner's written answers.

How many marks would you gain? How many would you lose? Try to work out why you lost marks.

1. Disability and its effects on those who are disabled and non-disabled/selfish people/lack of concern for others/the (unexpected) problems faced by disabled people/dangers for disabled people/lack of proper facilities for disabled people.

2. In the early part of the poem the narrator describes events at a distance/he is physically separated from the old man/he is closer now/he is touching the old man/talking to the old man.

Repetition: 'inch by inch' painfully slowly.

Word choice: 'drift' uncoordinated.

Simile: 'like a landscape'. The area is amplified as if he is crossing expanses of land.

List of the man's hazards: 'spilt sugar', 'slidy puddle', 'table edges', 'people's feet', 'slow dangerous inches'.

List of the man's perceptions: 'hiss', 'hamburgers', 'wet coats'.

Become an examiner (groups of four)

Re-read the last thirteen lines of the poem, then create three questions of your own. These might be on:

- Understanding (of the extract)
- Analysis (of the techniques used in the extract and their effects)
- Evaluation (of the impact of their effectiveness on the reader)

You should also create a marking scheme.

Themes

These are the main **concerns** of the text – the **issues** raised in it. They represent why the writer chose to write it to draw the **wider aspects** of the text to the attention of readers.

Read the themes below. Then try to identify specific parts of the text that show the theme being examined.

- Disabled people in society. Do we do enough to help them?
- Their dependence on wider society.
- Their steadfast refusal to give in to fate.
- The difficulties faced by disabled people.
- The lack of real communication between the rest of us and people who are disabled.

TQE exercise

Techniques	Effects
word choice	used to gain our sympathy for the old man
word order	used to slow down the action
repetition	to evoke sympathy for the man as the difficulty of his movements is described
caesura	to slow the action to put us in the old man's position
allusion	Christ
imagery	creates sympathy for the old man. Simile: 'like a monstrous animal caught in a tent'. Shows the views of others in the snack-bar.
narrative stance	We, as readers, realise that he is in a terrible condition. As such, we feel sorry for him as we see the events, not through their eyes, but through the eyes of the more humane observer/narrator. The poem starts in the third person then shades into the use of the first person in line 16 to show the narrator's gradual interest being absorbed by the events and the man. At first detached, he is later sympathetic to the old man's plight. The attitude of the narrator changes as the poem develops from pathos and empathy to admiration and this tracks the journey of the reader through the poem as we absorb his growing emotional attachment to the man.

Now, in pairs, find examples of these techniques from any part of the poem and write their effects using the TQE technique you used earlier. Remember, this stands for: Technique, Quotation, Explanation/Effect. Here is an example to get you started:

Word choice is often used by Morgan to gain the sympathy of the audience for the man in the poem (T). In line 4 for example, he uses the words 'old man' and 'trying to get to his feet' (Q). It is not a 'young' man who is struggling to find his feet; it is an 'old' man. Our automatic reaction, normally, would be to hurry to the aid of the man as the idea of supporting the weak, frail or elderly is simply part of our moral DNA. In addition to this, the poet's use of the present participle 'trying' conveys the idea that we are watching the process of the man's attempts to regain his footing and that he is not being entirely successful. He is struggling. Who will help? (E)

Question

The 8-mark question

By referring closely to this text and at least one other poem by Morgan, show how he creates characters with whom we sympathise. (8 marks)

You can answer this kind of question in bullet points, or write a number of linked statements, or even write a mini essay, although our recommendation is that you use bullets as this can be done more quickly under examination conditions.

Key words in the question:

The identification of **effective language techniques** to create **characters** with whom we **sympathise**.

Up to 2 marks can be achieved for identifying elements of **commonality** as identified in the question. A further 2 marks can be achieved for **reference to the extract given.** An additional 4 marks can be awarded for similar references to **at least one other text/part of the text** by the writer; so, 2+2+4 = 8 marks.

Let's begin by looking at the most likely poems to choose for this question. Which **two** would you choose?

Thinking aloud ...

'In the Snack-bar' is the chosen text so you have to find at least one other. 'Trio' certainly contains characters with whom we might sympathise. Although 'Good Friday' contains a character, it might be difficult to argue that he is worthy of sympathy, although it is certainly possible.

Let's stick with 'In the Snack-bar' and 'Trio'.

What techniques are used in the extract to gain our sympathy for the disabled man? Write these down.

Now think about 'Trio'. What techniques are used to draw our sympathies for the trio?

Examples of a bullet point approach and a mini essay approach are given below, but don't read through them until you have completed these tasks.

Bullet point approach

'In the Snack-bar'

Some suggestions (Any FOUR for 4 marks)

By referring closely to this text and at least one other poem by Morgan, show how he uses language effectively to create a character(s) with whom we sympathise.

- The man is so frail, he has to be helped to the toilet. Emphasised in the simple sentence, 'I take his arm.'
- Word choice: 'take' shows the power of the narrator and the lack of such power on the part of the old man. Or 'clings', which suggests the old man's desperation.
- Punctuation: 'Give me – your arm – it's better,' also shows his frailty as he gets more support/balance this way.
- Imagery/simile: 'A few yards of floor are like a landscape' shows how even the simplest things are amplified for the man because of his condition.
- Point of view is used to put the narrator (and us) in the position of the old man, who is concerned with the smallest things as they can all harm him: 'spilt sugar' on which he can slip, or 'table edges' on which he can injure himself, or even 'people's feet' on which he might trip.
- Metaphor of journey/biblical imagery to the toilet is like Christ's journey to Calvary. Also a symbol of the journey through life.

Bullet point approach

'Trio'

Some suggestions (Any FOUR for 4 marks)

By referring closely to this text and at least one other poem by Morgan, show how he uses language effectively to create a character(s) with whom we sympathise.

- Imagery of light, 'the Christmas lights' adds cheer and contrasts with the dark night.
- Word choice: The man is 'young' and the women are also young, 'a girl'. They have their whole lives in front of them.
- Humour: Their 'gifts'. These make us like them. The guitar to play music and cheer people up. The little dog in its brightly coloured coat and the Christmas baby, a symbol of new life.
- Allusion: 'a young man and two girls' are compared to the Magi. Metaphor of journey. Also a symbol of the journey through life.
  OR
  'the girl on the inside carries a very young baby,' also refers to the birth of Christ and conveys sympathy through word choice. The baby is 'very young', a newborn.
  Metaphor of their collective breath forming one single form, 'a cloud of happiness'.
- The pattern to follow in each case is a TQE structure:
  Point out the **technique** ... **Quote** an example ... **Explain** its use

Mini essay approach

In the poem 'In the Snack-bar', Morgan uses a variety of techniques to gain our sympathy for the main character, a disabled older man.

One such technique is that of using a simple sentence. This direct, uncomplicated way of describing the action indicates that the old man is so frail that he has to be helped to the toilet. In other words, he needs help with even the most basic of human needs.

Word choice emphasises the power of the narrator in the use of the active verb, 'take'. The opposite of this is also shown in another apposite word choice in the use of 'clings', which shows that the old man is very feeble.

Typically, Morgan also makes use of typography in order to press his theme, as the punctuation is also used to convey the frailty of the old man as he gets more support when he actually takes the arm of the narrator. His halting speech, too, draws our sympathy and this is emphasised through the use of the dashes: 'Give me – your arm – it's better'.

A simile, too, is used to demonstrate how even the simplest things are amplified for the old man because of his condition, making us feel sorry for him and so 'a few yards of floor are like a landscape'.

Morgan tries to put us in the position of the old man to appreciate his situation more clearly, so point of view is used to put the narrator (and us) in the position of the old man who is concerned with the smallest things as they can all harm him: 'spilt sugar' on which he can slip, or 'table edges' on which he can injure himself, or even 'people's feet' on which he might trip.

Finally, the metaphor of journey and the use of biblical imagery to describe the trip to the toilet is like Christ's journey to Calvary. It could also be a symbol of the journey through life. As Christ died for our sins in Christian belief, we the readers feel sympathy towards the man.

The metaphor of biblical journey is also used in 'Trio' in which 'a young man and two girls' are compared to the Magi who travelled to bring gifts to Christ. Our sympathies are also gained for the group as 'the girl on the inside carries a very young baby' which also refers to the birth of Christ and conveys sympathy through word choice. The baby is also 'very young'. In other words, it is a newborn.

Unlike 'In the Snack-bar', 'Trio' makes use of humour to gather sympathy for the trio of friends; their 'gifts' make us like them: the guitar to play music and cheer people up; the little dog in its brightly coloured coat; and the Christmas baby, a symbol of new life.

Like 'In the Snack-bar', 'Trio' uses imagery to draw out our sympathies. The trio bring light to an otherwise dark night. Under 'the Christmas lights' they add cheer to an otherwise cold night.

Word choice too is used to gain our sympathies. The man is 'young' and the women are also young, 'a girl'. In other words, they have their whole lives in front of them.

Finally, imagery is used (metaphor rather than simile this time) to create the impression of their collective breath forming one single form, 'a cloud of happiness' demonstrating that they are bonded together as friends, gaining our sympathies for them again.

Task

Write your own comment boxes in which you make three improvements to this mini essay.

'Good Friday'

In the last poem, we compared the old man's journey to that of Christ travelling to Calvary to be crucified on the Friday before Easter Sunday. This is the day on which Morgan has chosen to set this next poem. Specifically, it is set at exactly three o'clock, the hour at which Christ is thought to have died on the cross.

Task

What is the connection between the title and the poem?

Textual explosion!

This way of adding notes to a text helps you to figure out how it works.

Read the opening section of the poem and the comment boxes on the next page.

'Good Friday'

The time is too specific to be anything other than an ironic reference to the title. We expect a solemn religious content, but get the drunken ramblings of a man instead. Christians would be celebrating Christ's Passion at this point.

Three o'clock. The bus lurches

Word choice is appropriate. The sound of the word recreates the movement felt as the bus changes gears and turns a corner.

The bus and the drunk man move in a similar way, wavering on their (almost separate) journeys.

round into the sun. 'D's this go –'

Use of Glaswegian/Scots further helps to set the scene. Use of punctuation also recreates the slurred speech. The shortening of 'does' lengthens the sound of the 's' and the word 'this' becomes onomatopoeic, with the 'th' and 's' sounds adding to the slurring effect. The final dash shows the end of the speech as the man has to focus his attention on sitting down.

Dashes are significant here. They show the flow of the conversation is being interrupted.

The narrator is introduced as a fellow (sober) traveller. We, as readers, can sympathise as we may have been in this situation. It was not uncommon in Glasgow in the past.

he flops beside me – 'right along Bath Street?

Word choice. Uncontrolled. Not in full control of his movements. Gravity and the movement of the bus have seated him. He would also disturb the fellow passenger.

The question, started before he sat down, is now finished. Very rude.

– Oh tha's, tha's all right, see I've

The question does not appear to be answered by the narrator, perhaps trying to ignore the man, or he immediately answers his own question. The slurring continues with the shortened and repeated, 'tha's' shows his state of inebriation. He may also have retracted his question before the narrator has a chance to answer.

Easter eggs represent the stone covering the cave in which Christ's body was buried and from which he rose again after death. This is the central event in Christianity as it proved his Godhood. This astonishing event has been reduced to eggs being bought for children in this man's eyes. This is its significance now.

got to get some Easter eggs for the kiddies.

His reason for being here is explained and is even more incongruous with the title and man's condition – buying Easter eggs. This links again to the title.

Task

Now you try to do the same, in pairs, with the next ten lines of the poem from, 'I've had a wee drink ...' to 'see what I mean?'

You might wish to comment on some of the techniques identified already, such as the use of word choice, dashes, understatement, irony and repetition. Use the TQE technique. The first one has been done for you.

Technique	Quotation	Explanation
Line 6 Understatement	'wee drink'	Ironic effect – he's had much more than a small amount to drink
Line 7 Irony	'funny day'	
Line 8 Word choice	'celebrating'	
Lines 9–10 Repetition		
Lines 13–16 Dashes		

Commentary

In the next section of the poem, the drunk man mentions his lack of education and he uses this to justify his lack of understanding of Easter. His circular journey, like Christ's own journey to Calvary, ends with him leaving the bus unsteadily, heading 'into the sun'.

Is the drunk man pretending to be more ignorant than he actually is in order to provoke a response from the speaker?

The drunk man develops his earlier tactic by reinforcing the perceived differences between working class and the 'educatit' class – another theme of the poem.

Irony again. Is he genuinely unable to put his thoughts into words or does he manage this successfully? Morgan himself was born and bred in Rutherglen. Do we need this divide between working and educated classes?

Irony as the man doesn't realise the significance of the outburst. Also generates humour.

rose fae the dead like, see what I mean?

You're an educatit man, you can tell me –

– Aye, well. There ye are. It's been seen

time and again, the working man

has nae education, he jist canny – jist

hasny got it, know what I mean,

he's jist bliddy ignorant – Christ aye,

bliddy ignorant. Well –' The bus brakes violently,

he lunges for the stair, swings down – off,

into the sun for his Easter eggs,

on very

      nearly

          steady

            legs.

The man backs down as the bus brakes. The typography (the punctuation) is used to show this.

Return to English, bus goes from lurching to breaking 'violently' – possibly a reference to the emotional state of the drunk man, beginning light-hearted and humorous and finishing in a very self-defeating, deflated manner.

The typographical layout physically looks like the stairs on a double decker bus. The reader is forced to slow their reading, which makes us think of how slowly and carefully the man must exit the bus because of his condition.

The man's ignorance is reinforced as he focuses only on the material side of Easter.

Research

What were the main stages in Christ's journey to Calvary? What are the similarities to the journey in this poem? What are the differences?

Read the next section on themes and techniques and then try to show where these themes/techniques appear in the poem specifically.

Themes

- Education
- Working class versus educated 'middle' class
- English versus Scots
- The role of alcohol in Scottish society
- Religion

Techniques

Word choice: use of Scots versus Standard English.

Punctuation: used to stop and start the conversation to mimic both the man's fractured speech and the stop–start motion of the bus.

Irony: Christ's journey to Calvary was punctuated by stops as he tried to recover his strength for the next phase of the journey. This was the reality of the Passion. The man's journey is very different, although his destination is Bath Street, which is one of the highest points in Glasgow. This suggests that the direction of travel was upwards.

Symbolism: references to the sun could be literal as they drive into the sunshine. It was also reported that when Christ died on the cross, the former bright sunshine turned to darkness. The reference could also refer to the son of God, that is, Christ himself.

Typography: concerns anything on the page except the words. The layout of the last four lines actually looks like the stairs of a bus.

Repetition: to suggest the man's drunkenness.

Narrative stance: on the surface, this is a drunken conversation, but we realise that the narrator never replies. As such, it is really a monologue, an account of the man's reflections spoken to himself, as if he is having a conversation with himself on the journey.

'Trio'

The third poem in the collection, 'Trio', shares a similar setting to those already covered – Glasgow and specifically, Buchanan Street with its bustling shops. The setting in time is never given for 'In the Snack-bar', but there is a very specific setting for 'Good Friday' (Easter) and for 'Trio' – Christmas.

The religious thread is clear through all three poems. In the case of 'Trio', the theme is of celebration, ironically, because religion does not matter – the message is that we should take pleasure in the simple things in life.

Morgan uses the motif of journey in all three poems. In this case, the journey reminds us of that of the Magi – the three wise men who travelled to Bethlehem to bring gifts to the newborn Christ. These have been replaced by one man and two young women. Their 'gifts' are not the gold, frankincense and myrrh of the biblical story, but a guitar, a very young baby and a chihuahua.

Task

Don't look at the answers below. What does the title of the poem makes us think of?

- The number three, which suggests completeness in Hebrew thinking
- A musical trio
- The Holy Trinity of Father, Son and Holy Spirit

The word order is altered in the opening lines:

'Coming up Buchanan Street, quickly, on a sharp evening

A young man and two girls,'

The normal order would be:

'A young man and two girls [are] coming up Buchanan Street, quickly, on a sharp evening,'

The changed order emphasises their movement up Buchanan Street. This is further emphasised by the adverb 'quickly', as they are trying to stay warm because it is a 'sharp evening'.

The sentence structures are then repeated with some variation in the lines:

'The young man carries a new guitar in his arms,

the girl on the inside carries a very young baby,

and the girl on the outside carries a chihuahua.'

The perspective/point of view is of a narrator observing events in the present from higher up Buchanan Street as the trio approaches him/her.

Mood/tone is boisterous:

'Wait till he sees this but!'

The three are clearly on their way to visit someone. This is revealed as they pass the narrator and continue to climb Buchanan Street. They all have things to show 'him' – the person they are visiting.

Textual explosion!

This way of adding notes to a text helps you to figure out how it works.

Read the opening section of the poem and the comment boxes below.

'Trio'

Cold and warmth, as well as dark and light, are contrasted.

Coming up Buchanan Street, quickly, on a sharp evening

a young man and two girls, under the Christmas lights –

'Under the Christmas' suggests they are being observed/protected. Christmas represents the birth of Jesus. The Magi – the three wise men – followed a star [Christmas lights]. Again, the idea of a current journey paralleling a biblical one is important in this poem as is the idea of the religious and the material.

Links back to the idea of a musical trio and reminds us of the wise men bearing gifts for Jesus.

The young man carries a new guitar in his arms,

the girl on the inside carries a very young baby,

Reminds us again of Jesus, drawing parallels between present and past.

The travellers carry gifts, but they are different from those of the wise men. They are modern gifts and full of life – literally in the case of the baby. The little dog is clearly a gift for someone, who will plainly be delighted.

and the girl on the outside carries a chihuahua.

And the three of them are laughing, their breath rises

Their breath has become one thing and rises to heaven almost as a visual prayer – something tangible you can see.

The earlier metaphor is developed into the idea of a cloud of joy – again a fitting prayer at this time of the year.

in a cloud of happiness, and as they pass

the boy says, 'Wait till he sees this but!'

The chihuahua has a tiny Royal Stewart tartan coat like a teapot–holder,

Continues idea of the past and present, the high and the low, the serious and the fun. Alludes to the Stewart kings of Scotland and exemplifies the two sides to Christmas. Simile contrasts with the grandeur of the old Scottish kings.

Focus shifts to the second gift – the baby. White symbolises purity and innocence. The technique of synecdoche is used as the eyes and mouth are used to describe the whole baby – it is full of life and joy. Simile is then used to compare the baby's features to wedding cake decorations, again taking up the idea of celebration.

the baby in its white shawl is all bright eyes and mouth like favours

in a fresh sweet cake,

the guitar swells out under its milky plastic cover, tied at the neck

The third gift – the guitar. Swelling suggests 'pregnancy' or birth and the milky plastic cover links back to the baby. Together the images suggest life and vibrancy – the end of one year and the beginning of another.

with silver tinsel tape and a brisk sprig of mistletoe.

Another example of the juxtaposition of the grand with the ordinary, but this time the reference is to classical Greek mythology as opposed to the Bible. These lines are all about love. Orpheus rescued his lover Eurydice from Hell in the past, while in the present both baby and dog are well loved, too.

Orphean sprig! Melting baby! Warm chihuahua!

The vale of tears is powerless before you.

Ironic reversal. Biblical metaphor for life's problems, yet it is powerless before the joy of life.

This is the real message of the poem. Whether we believe in God or not, simple joy and happiness put us in charge of our own fate.

Whether Christ is born, or is not born, you

put paid to fate, it abdicates

under the Christmas lights.

After alluding to the Bible and Greek legend, Morgan describes the day-to-day trials of life as 'monsters'.

Monsters of the year

Military imagery is used now to show the defeat of the life's trials.

go blank, are scattered back,

can't bear this march of three.

The perspective, until this point, has been of an observer looking down at the approaching trio. They have now reached and passed the narrator.

– And the three have passed, vanished in the crowd

The military imagery is now developed into the idea of a shield of laughter that protects them against life's challenges.

(yet not vanished, for in their arms they wind

the life of men and beasts, and music,

laughter ringing them round like a guard)

at the end of this winter's day.

Scottish text questions

Read the questions below and then the sample responses. Finally, judge, in pairs, how well they answer the questions.

Questions

1. In lines 6 and 7, an atmosphere of happiness is created. How is this continued in lines 8–10?
2. What are the themes of this poem as expressed in lines 16–19?

Possible answers

1. The exclamation mark at the end of the expression, 'Wait till he sees this but!'

   - Word order. Placing 'but' at the end of the sentence adds to the excitement.
   - Use of colloquial language conveys happiness as he thinks about the reaction his gift will bring.
   - The image of the chihuahua, a tiny dog, with its equally tiny tartan coat, makes the reader (and perhaps the narrator) smile.
   - Bright colours of the 'Royal Stewart' tartan.
   - The incongruity of the 'Royal' tartan on such a small dog.

2. The 'vale of tears' is a metaphor for the challenges life throws at us. Morgan is arguing that in the face of this trio, life's tribulations are weak and 'powerless'. As such, they 'abdicate[s]' or resign in the face of the joy and happiness of the trio. Here, fate or life's difficulties are likened to a king who gives up his throne.

Task

Try this next task in pairs.

1. Using your own words, explain the meaning of lines 20–27.
2. Now turn to Chapter 5 for a sample critical essay on 'Trio' with comments. Again in pairs, use the supplementary marking grid on pages 165–66 to grade this piece of writing and to evaluate its strengths. What are its main strengths? Provide **two** areas for improvement. Specifically refer to each part of the marking grid to justify your mark. Once you have done the task, read the expert commentary on page 152.

Possible answers

1. Life's challenges have been described as abdicating kings. They are now seen as mythical monsters. Like the monsters of myth, who are often defeated by heroes (like Orpheus earlier in the poem), fate has no response to the trio. It goes 'blank'. After this, it is 'scattered back' like a defeated army, as it is unable to withstand, ironically, the 'march of three'.

   At this point, the trio passes the narrator and has 'vanished' in the crowd of Christmas shoppers. The reason the narrator appears to contradict himself in the next line is that they have not vanished from memory.

   Laughter, joy, happiness and camaraderie will protect us from everything the world has to throw at us is the message/theme.

Task

Each of the poems so far has made use of an internal narrator – someone who takes part in or observes or reports the actions in the poem. Write a brief outline of the main effects of the use of this device in each of the three poems. You may wish to have a scan through the commentary below to start you off.

'Winter'

'Winter' begins the second group of poems in this collection dealing with the topic of places.

Commentary

The next poem in the collection, 'Winter', is set in winter. It, too, has a Glasgow setting – Bingham's pond near Great Western Road and next to the Pond hotel.

In common with many of Morgan's poems, the narrative voice is distanced from the occurring events, a kind of detached passer-by, thus allowing objective commentary, which allows him/her to reflect on the passing scenes.

The poem is a description of a pond scene. It makes reference to swans, the pond itself, woods and then shifts focus to the dual carriageway while finally ending with the narrator in his/her room considering the changing scenery of the pond.

The main theme is about decay, the passage of time and its effects on the natural world.

The key symbol is the use of the Bingham's pond as an enduring rural landscape within a cityscape as it has been in existence for around 130 years, yet by the end of the poem it too is subject to change.

Textual explosion!

This way of adding notes to a text helps you to figure out how it works.

Read the opening section of the poem and the comment boxes below.

'Winter'

The year goes, the woods decay, and after,

many a summer dies. The swan

> Bingham's pond is on Great Western Road, Glasgow near the Pond hotel.

on Bingham's pond, a ghost, comes and goes.

> The swan is literally moving across the ice and is metaphorically a ghost as it is fleeting and because of the shared colour.

It goes, and ice appears, it holds,

> Alliteration 'stand … surprised', 'bears boys'. Sound is also used in 'skates', 'take' and 'tracks' to recreate the sound of skating on ice.

bears gulls that stand around surprised,

blinking in the heavy light, bears boys

when skates take over swan-tracks gone.

> Repeats the word in line 2 with a little variation. Double meaning. Could relate to death and colour changes. The colours of summer and the colours of winter.

After many summer dyes, the swan-white ice

glints only crystal beyond white. Even

dearest blue's not there, though poets would find it.

$\rightarrow$

I find one stark scene

> Human noises now enter the scene. This is a poem that is both visual and auditory. Note the sharpness of the consonants – 'stark … scene … cut … cries'. Describes the harshness of this winterscape.

cut by evening cries, by warring air.

> Deviant collocation. Suggests that the wind is violently blowing in all directions, as if fighting itself. Onomatopoeia on warring. Sounds like a fierce wind.

The muffled hiss of blades escapes into breath,

hangs with it a moment, fades off.

> Here, Morgan refers to the language of drama. 'Fades … scene', and reference to voices fading in and out suggests that changing season is like a play or film. Again, visuals and sounds are of key significance in conveying the theme of change.

Fades off, goes, the scene, the voices fade,

> Lexical sets. These words all perform the same function. 'Fall, decay … break … disappear'. The idea is of change and decay.

the line of trees, the woods that fall, decay

and break, the dark comes down, the shouts

run off into it and disappear.

> Now we shift to the human world which is changing too with light fading. Fog is personified as a human driver heading to the west of Scotland. The fog literally looks like a monster. Shifting grammatical categories. Monstrous is placed in an adverbial position in the sentence, but functions as a adjective. Could also be transferred epithet referring to fog.

At last the lamps go too, when fog

drives monstrous down the dual carriageway

> Internal narrator is used again as detached observer.

out to the west, and even in my room

> Repeated use of the words 'grey' and 'dead' represent the death of summer as season changes to winter.

and on this paper I do not know

about that grey dead pane

of ice that sees nothing and that nothing sees.

Questions

Individual/homework activity

1. Google search the line, 'after many a summer dies. The swan ...' You should find the following: http://tinyurl.com/nfandxm
   Read the 'summary' section and then write a paragraph linking the reference to Tennyson's poem to this poem. Try to explain the connection(s).
2. What is the purpose of the reference to Bingham's pond?
3. Explain the metaphor of the swan being a ghost in lines 2–3.
4. Lines 1–10 describe the changes on the pond. In line 10, Morgan writes that 'blue's not there,' – meaning the blue of the water – and then adds that 'poets would find it.' What do you think this means?
5. Lines 11–18 describe 'a stark scene', raucous with the sounds of skating, of screaming voices, of 'warring air' where the vicious winter wind blows in all directions as if is in a war against itself. The scene then changes as time passes and darkness takes hold, 'the woods that fall', perhaps with the wind or with the passage of time, and the skaters go home.
   What technique is being used in the expression 'warring air'? What effect does it create? How effective is it?
6. The final sequence of the poem in lines 19–24 shifts the scene towards the 'dual carriageway' and even details the end of or changes to that more urban landscape with its 'lamps' which are being changed by the all-encroaching fog. The poem ends with the narrator's pessimistic musings about things ending in a pitiless way over which we have no control.
   In lines 19–20, Morgan uses a technique to describe the fog. Name the technique and describe its effects.

'Slate'

'Slate' shares similarities with the previous poem, 'Winter'. It is also different in terms of its structure which is very well-defined in this poem, unlike all of the other poems in this collection. It is a sonnet.

Sonnet

Sonnets contain 14 lines. This one is based on a sonnet known as the Petrarchan sonnet. It was named after a Renaissance Italian poet who often wrote of his unrequited love for a lady named Laura. It has a particular rhyme scheme: ABBA CDDC EFG EFG.

It can be broken down into two parts: the octet (the first eight lines) and the sestet (the final six lines).

The octet is further broken down into two quatrains (two sets of four lines). In each quatrain, the first and fourth lines rhyme and the second and third lines also rhyme.

The function of the octet is often to present an issue to the reader in the first quatrain and then to develop it in the second.

The sestet contains two tercets (sets of three lines). The function of the sestet is often to comment on the issue arising in the octet and possibly to apply a solution to it.

The first sestet has another name – the *volta*, which is Italian for 'turn'.

Textual explosion!

This way of adding notes to a text helps you to figure out how it works.

Read the opening section of the poem and the comment boxes below.

'Slate'

Octet

Quatrain 1

> Irony because it is the beginning of this poem. Short sentence stops the reader, making them think of the notion that is being suggested – that there is no beginning to life/world as it has always existed.

There is no beginning. We saw Lewis (A)

> Locates the scene away from the urban settings of the last three to the island of Lewis. We is the first person plural suggesting that there is no single narrator. The voice here is collective. To whom does it belong? Ancestors? Is it like a Greek chorus acting as commentator on events others cannot see?

> Word choice suggests that care has been taken over the placing of the island. The alliteration adds to the idea of a lightness and delicacy about the handling. There is a slight contradiction, however, as, if there is no beginning then how has it come about that Lewis has been witnessed being laid down?

laid down, when there was not much but thunder (B)

and volcanic fires; watched long seas plunder (B)

faults; laughed as Staffa cooled. Drumlins blue as (A)

> Imagery and two similes are used. Drumlins are oval-shaped hills formed under glaciers. They are described as 'blue as bruises' to convey their colour and the violence of their birth. Again, an unpleasant environment, devoid of human life. Note that the sense crosses from quatrain 1 to quatrain 2.

> The environment at the beginning is hostile and savage. Raw energy. Basic elements. Earth. Air. Fire. Water. Is there a cruelty about the narrators who laughed as Staffa cooled? Their perspective is god-like, similar to pre-Christian Titans.

Quatrain 2

> Imagery – 'grated' – sharp and violent action. Small pieces of the drumlin are being shred off the landscape. Nutmegs are being compared to the drumlins. The nutmegs are small and fragile compared to the grater, just as the drumlins are fragile compared to mother nature who is changing the landscape.

bruises were grated off like nutmegs; bens, (C)

and a great glen, gave a rough back we like (D)

to think the ages must streak, surely strike, (D)

seldom stroke, but raised and shaken, with tens (C)

> Alliteration – repetition of the letter 's' provides these lines with a quicker rhythm that reflects the passing of time: 'ages'.

Sestet

Tercet 1

of thousands of rains, blizzards, sea-poundings (E)

shouldered off into night and memory. (F)

Memory of men! That was to come. Great (G)

Tercet 2

in their empty hunger these surroundings (E)

threw walls to the sky, the sorry glory (F)

of a rainbow. Their heels kicked flint, chalk, slate. (G)

> Word choice: their hunger is said to be empty suggesting that is it not a real hunger or need that they have.

> Oxymoron: the notion of apologetic praise contradicts one another. There is praise for the rainbow, suggesting the rains and thunder have ceased. This is significant because although the rain has stopped, there is regret for leaving the past behind and moving on to a new age.

Carousel activity – this is where groups contribute collaboratively to the outcome of a task. In this case, each group will 'carousel' around each stanza/part to build a detailed picture of the poet's purpose in each one. Divide the class into groups of four. Each group should deal with each stanza/part to allow for ideas to build.

1. What problem/issue is raised in the first quatrain?
2. Is it developed in the second quatrain?
3. Is there a 'turn' evident in the first tercet?
4. Is there a resolution in the final tercet?

Homework

There is also another sonnet form known as the English sonnet.

Research it online. How is it different from the Italian form?

'Hyena'

Initial thoughts

A poem's title often builds an expectation as to what its content will be about. Sometimes there is a clear connection between the title and its content; sometimes there are surprises!

'Hyena' is written as a dramatic monologue in the first person, and in the present tense. This form of poetry often makes unexpected revelations about the character being explored and this is certainly the case with the hyena.

Textual explosion!

This way of adding notes to a text helps you to figure out how it works.

Read the opening section of the poem and the comment boxes on the next page.

'Hyena'

Section 1

Connotations of evil. A sinister animal. Savage. Loud, hysterical laughter, as if crazed. A scavenger. Hateful. Disliked.

First person narrative mode used throughout the poem allowing the inner thoughts of the speaker (the hyena of the title) to be voiced. Disturbing image. To whom is it addressed? Readers? Prey? Tone established is of latent/nascent threat.

I am waiting for you.

Unusual collocation. Likened to a human traveller. The purpose behind this travel, however, is not sightseeing. Irony.

I have been travelling all morning through the bush

and not eaten.

Hunger is its driving force. We gather this by implication.

Mirrors the sentence structure of the opening line: subject – present participle verb. These stretch out time to show its patience/determination/resolve. 'Waiting', 'travelling', 'lying' form lexical sets. They all perform the same role – to draw out time.

I am lying at the edge of the bush

Image of a desolate, isolated and abandoned place. A kraal is an enclosure for keeping animals. The traces of civilisation have gone.

on a dusty path that leads from the burnt-out kraal.

Two comma splices in one short line. There should be three sentences here. The effect is to create the idea of the continuous movement of events and time suggesting growing desperation in this dry, arid, deadly environment.

I am panting, it is midday, I found no water-hole.

I am very fierce without food and although my eyes

are screwed to slits against the sun

you must believe I am prepared to spring.

Word choice suggests the animal is dangerous, further adding to the tone of threat and intimidation. This line tells the reader that this animal is always watching, waiting and prepared to attack its prey.

Section 2

Use of rhetorical question astonishes the reader. Inviting observation. False pride? Or posed to allow reader to gauge the hyena's true nature rather than the public image.

What do you think of me?

Answers his own question. Arrogance? Simile compares its exterior to the African continent. The commonality? Roughness. It is a tough animal in a tough landscape.

I have a rough coat like Africa.

Word choice. builds the image of a sly, methodical hunter.

I am crafty with dark spots ← 'Dark' could suggest evil.

Second landscape simile building on the earlier comparison. Fairly exact. Coat is rough and in tufts. Again the animal identifies with its environment; is in harmony with it.

like the bush-tufted plains of Africa.

Simile compares the hyena to raw potential energy just waiting to be released.

I sprawl as a shaggy bundle of gathered energy

Second simile compares the hyena again to the continent.

like Africa sprawling in its waters.

Repetitive simple sentence structures with variation in the verbs. Omission of full stops to suggest continuous action. Lexical sets 'trot' and 'lope' convey the movements. Final sentence personifies the animal as a hunter.

I trot, I lope, I slaver, I am a ranger.

Short, sharp sentence has impact when placed at the end of this section, reminding the reader that the hyena feasts on dead animals unflinchingly. 'I hunch my shoulders.'

I hunch my shoulders. I eat the dead.

Section 3

Echoes the opening of section 2. Rhetorical question. This question changes the topic of the monologue and thus lightens the mood of the poem.

The repetition of 'and' slows the pace of the poem and adds to the more romantic tone of this stanza. The idea of the hyena on his solo nocturnal ventures.

Do you like my song?

When the moon pours hard and cold on the veldt

I sing, and I am the slave of darkness.

Over the stone walls and the mud walls and the ruined places

→

and the owls, the moonlight falls.

> There is both visual and auditory imagery here. Moonlight and the silver pelt=visual. The hyena's song=auditory. Creates a much more romantic image which contrasts with the earlier sterile images of dead, dusty plains.

I sniff a broken drum. I bristle. My pelt is silver.

> This image of the hyena howling to the moon likens the creature to a wolf – perhaps showing what he would like to become and showing a self-loathing for his own species.

I howl my song to the moon – up it goes.

> Tone of threat and menace returns with this question, the false sense of security created in stanza 3 is shattered with this line. A dangerous animal.

Would you meet me there in the waste places?

Section 4

It is said I am a good match   Self-disparaging irony. Not really a good hunter. A scavenger.

for a dead lion. I put my muzzle

> Contrasting colour imagery. Lion is gold. Hyena is silver. Inferior.

at his golden flanks, and tear. He

is my golden supper, but my tastes are easy.

> Deviant collocation. Crowd of fangs. Vampiric idea of draining life.

I have a crowd of fangs, and I use them.

> Use of 'lolling' and 'long' and 'tongue' helps to simulate the action of the tongue rolling, hungrily, out of its mouth. Sinister end. The hyena appears to be laughing, but it is an evil snarl rather than a laugh.

Oh and my tongue – do you like me

when it comes lolling out over my jaw

very long, and I am laughing?

I am not laughing.   Definitive answer to the question. Hyena reminds the reader that he is a killer, whose instinct is to survive on the death of others – irony.

But I am not snarling either, only

panting in the sun, showing you

what I grip   Dead animals. Displaying his kill, prey, meat proudly – the theme of death is emphasised.

carrion with.

Section 5

I am waiting ◄——— Irony. Hyena waits for death in order to sustain his own life.

Repetition of 'for' builds the momentum and pace of the poem – the tone become increasingly tense as the poem reaches its climax.

for the foot to slide,

for the heart to seize,

for the leaping sinews to go slack,

for the fight to the death to be fought to the death, ◄——— The repetition and balance of the words in this sentence are used to show the fine balance between life and death. Lengthening sentences show the hyena nearing his prey.

for a glazing eye and the rumour of blood.

Sinister and disconcerting image that the hyena is always watching and waiting for prey. Desecrating the remains of the dead – particularly eerie and threatening image. The poem ends on the image and theme of death – strong suggestion that the dead will return to dust and become part of the land, sea and wind, becoming part of Africa.

I am crouching in my dry shadows

till you are ready for me.

My place is to pick you clean

and leave your bones to the wind.

Questions

1. What do you know about hyenas?
2. Now re-read the first line of the poem. What are the surprises?
3. What unexpected facts are we made aware of in lines 1–9?
4. Stanza 2 in lines 10–17 sees the hyena compared to many things. Identify them and the effects of each comparison.
5. Stanza 3 in lines 18–25 begins unusually; in what way(s)? The last line in this section is sinister – explain why.
6. Stanza 4 in lines 26–38 continues the character exploration. There are clearly two sides to the hyena. Describe them.
7. Stanza 5 in lines 39–48 gives the impression that the attention of the hyena is now focused on the reader. How does Morgan achieve this effect?

Thematic mapping using Venn diagrams

In order to complete the final 8-mark question in the textual analysis part of the examination paper, you need to be able to identify the connections or commonality between some of the different poems in the collection. The question rubric usually asks you to consider an aspect(s) of the poem and then show how this/these relate(s) to at least one more poem by the same author. These 'maps' will help you to do this.

Now that you have read all of the poems, you need to complete each circle as fully as you can by using the carousel technique. This will mean dividing the class into groups of four. Each should then add as much information as possible for each of the poems.

Questions

Consider the following question:

With close textual reference, discuss in what ways this poem shares similar themes to one or more poems by Morgan.

Question analysis – three-way Venn diagram:

1. Write down the keywords in the question.
2. Assuming that 'In the Snack-bar' is the chosen text, which other(s) might you choose? Justify your answer.
3. Complete a Venn diagram to show the thematic similarities. The example below for 'In the Snack-bar' and 'Trio' has been started for you.

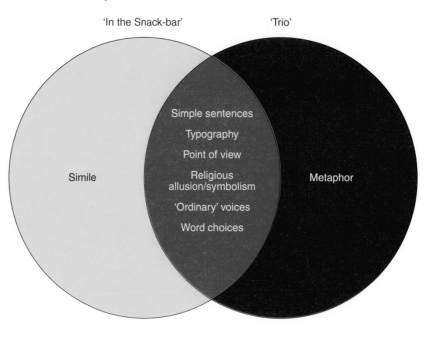

'In the Snack-bar'   'Trio'

Simile

Simple sentences
Typography
Point of view
Religious allusion/symbolism
'Ordinary' voices
Word choices

Metaphor

Creating Venn diagrams in Word

See the link below for help and advice:

http://tinyurl.com/na7s72t

Task

Use a three-way Venn diagram to show the similarities between 'Winter', 'Hyena' and 'Slate'.

INTRODUCTION:
WHAT DO I NEED TO KNOW ABOUT HIGHER?

The next two chapters are about writers who can be studied at either National 5 or Higher level: Iain Crichton Smith and Norman MacCaig. The activities are suitable for both National 5 and Higher and there are Higher alternatives to National 5 questions.

What are the differences between National 5 and Higher?

Texts

Most texts are specific to either National 5 or Higher BUT there are four 'crossover' writers/texts, two of which we will be looking at.

Question types

Most questions at Higher level are more demanding than those at National 5 – though some may look very similar.

Answers

What is expected at Higher is different from National 5. As a general rule, you will be expected to 'do more' for your marks at Higher level. How does this work in practice? Some of the differences are straightforward:

- At National 5, you will often see questions out of 2 marks (or multiples of 2). The 'model' here is: 1 mark for quote/reference/identify technique plus 1 mark for explanation.
- At Higher level, you will not usually gain a separate mark for quoting or referring to the text (though you will be expected to). Instead, you will gain 1 mark for 'quote and explain'. (There are no half marks in either of these parts.)
- Other differences may seem slightly more complicated. At Higher, you will usually be able to gain 2 marks for a 'detailed/insightful comment and reference' and 1 mark for 'more basic comment and reference'. If a question is out of 4 marks, you should be able to build up marks through 2+2, 2+1+1 or 1+1+1+1. There is flexibility built into the system of gaining marks, meaning you can be rewarded for the depth and detail of your comments as well as the number of comments you make: quality as well as quantity.

Marking of the final question in the Scottish text question: at Higher, this is worth 10 marks out of 20 (8 out of 20 at National 5). Why? Again, this makes Higher more challenging: there is greater emphasis on comments which go 'beyond' the extract, making links/comparisons. So, a more independent answer is required at Higher level. →

To sum up, the marks for the final question are divided:

- National 5 (total 8 marks): 2 (commonality – showing a general understanding of the aspect of the writer's work identified in the question) +2 (the extract) +4 (other texts)
- Higher (total 10 marks): 2 (commonality) +2 (extract) +6 (other texts)
- At Higher, the aim again is to reward quality of comment, not just quantity: 6 marks can be gained by 3x2 marks (3x2 marks per comment) or even 2x3 marks (2x3 marks per comment), depending on how detailed and insightful the comments are.
- The aim is to achieve flexibility and openness in how you can gain marks. And remember, it is possible to score 20/20!

CHAPTER 3
IAIN CRICHTON SMITH

Iain Crichton Smith is a brilliant, versatile writer, famous for his poetry and novels as well as short stories. He was born in Glasgow in 1928 and lived, when he was young, in a small Hebridean community, before settling in Oban, on the west coast of Scotland. Here he worked as a teacher and did not become a full-time writer until he retired. For many years he cared for his mother and married later in his life, after his mother's death.

Take a closer look

You can see Iain Crichton Smith discuss his life and work on YouTube:

http://tinyurl.com/nwe2crs

If you are studying Iain Crichton Smith for your National 5 or Higher Scottish text question, you will read six short stories from *The Red Door* collection – 'The Crater', 'In Church', 'The Telegram', 'Mother and Son', 'The Painter' and 'The Red Door.'

These stories can be divided into two groups, each of which deals with a major theme (with one story overlapping). These are:

War: 'The Crater', 'In Church', 'The Telegram'.

Conformity versus individuality in a small community: 'The Telegram' (again), 'Mother and Son', 'The Painter', 'The Red Door'.

There are other links that can be made between different stories in this selection. We will look at these after you have studied the stories in detail.

These stories deal with subjects Crichton Smith felt strongly about and had experienced, for example life in a small community, where everyone knows your business, and how difficult it is to be an individual in a world where you are expected to conform. He wrote about how complicated human relationships can be, even in close families. Crichton Smith lived through the Second World War (though too young to fight in it) and he wrote a number of stories about war and its horrifying effects on people. Above all, he cared about human beings and his stories deal with experiences and issues that are shared by many of us today.

As you progress through this section, you will move from preliminary activities to 'get you started' (for example, there are lots of tasks to do on 'The Crater', the first story) to more independent study and exam-style questions.

But, surely, short stories are just meant to be read and enjoyed as stories, aren't they? Well, yes and no.

'The Crater'

Look at the opening of 'The Crater', a story set in the trenches of the First World War.

> In the intervals of inaction it had been decided by the invisible powers that minor raids were feasible and therefore to be recommended. In the words of the directive: 'For reasons known to you we are for the moment acting on the defensive so far as serious operations are concerned but this should not preclude the planning of local attacks on a comparatively small scale ...'

We can see immediately that Crichton Smith is not just telling a story or describing a scene. He is doing something far more skilful and complex than that.

What does the opening tell us?

We are in a wartime setting. Although there is no major battle taking place, minor raids on the enemy trenches are allowed – in fact encouraged. We probably realise at this point that such a raid is going to happen in the story; and what about the title – 'The Crater'? A crater is a large hole in the ground, like the ones on the moon's surface. There were many mud-filled craters in 'no man's land' – the area between the two armies' trenches. They were caused by exploding artillery shells and were very dangerous: soldiers could fall in and drown. So, the title plus the opening paragraph might make us predict that this will be a story about a raid across no man's land, in which a crater is going to be important.

But there's more. Crichton Smith mentions the 'invisible powers' that sent out the 'directive' (official instruction) to the soldiers – that is, the 'high up' authorities in the army. What are the connotations of that word 'invisible', used to describe the army authorities? Not seen? Distant? Maybe not really interested in the soldiers? In that case, the directive to encourage 'minor raids' seems heartless, even sinister.

Crichton Smith follows this up by quoting the actual message sent from the invisible authorities: the fact that there is no major battle happening 'should not preclude (prevent) the planning of local attacks on a comparatively small scale …'

You might notice two things right away:

1. The formal style – words like 'preclude' and 'comparatively' – sounds unemotional and, considering raids can mean casualties, inhumane.
2. What is a 'small scale' attack in wartime? For every soldier involved in minor raids, there is the possibility of death – and the death of every soldier matters. Each death is a total tragedy for that soldier and his family – there is no such thing as an unimportant, 'small' death.

So, what does it all mean? The formal directive indicates that a 'local attack' is insignificant, but this idea is undermined by Crichton Smith's suggestion that the authorities' attitude is heartless. Dying in a minor raid is perhaps even worse than sacrificing your life in a battle to achieve something important – like saving other lives or fighting injustice – it seems even more pointless.

The next sentence of the story sees Lieutenant Robert Mackinnon preparing for a raid.

What can we predict?

There is going to be a raid – not significant in the eyes of the authorities – but which will matter to the soldiers involved. And there will be a crater.

If you have already read 'The Crater', you will know how close this prediction is!

If you haven't yet read it, now is the time …

Consolidating your knowledge of the story

The first important thing to do is consolidate your knowledge of the story: to make sure you know it confidently. To achieve this, we will divide the story up into different elements: plot, characters and theme – and we will analyse the writer's style, used to create all of these. Of course this is a bit artificial: in reality, we experience all of these elements together when we read and enjoy a story. However, to gain confident knowledge, it helps at first to focus on these elements separately.

Plot

This story, like all six from Crichton Smith, has – at first glance – a simple plot, which can be summed up in four sentences:

1. The soldiers go on a raid (**opening of the story – characters placed in a situation**).
2. Lieutenant Mackinnon leads a mission to search for Morrison, who is missing (**tension builds**).
3. They pull him out of the crater – but he dies anyway (**climax – the most dramatic or exciting part of the story**).
4. They walk back to the trench (**resolution – 'rounds off' the story**).

However, a thorough reading of the story reveals a lot of subtle action going on. We can see how Crichton Smith uses the events of the story to develop his characters and themes.

Task

Here is a more detailed summary of the plot. This time the sentences have been jumbled up. By 'unjumbling' them, you will develop your confident knowledge of the plot, which will help your study of other aspects of the story.

a) Lieutenant Robert Mackinnon prepares for a raid.
b) Back at the trench, they hear a cry of terrible despair, and go looking again.
c) Robert hangs over the edge, holding his rifle down like a 'rescue rope'.
d) They walk back to their own trench, carrying Morrison's body.
e) Robert finds Morrison – and is shocked by the horrifying sight of him.
f) Sergeant Smith's assessment of the rescue – and Mackinnon's behaviour – is mainly practical.
g) They shout into the crater for a second time.
h) Hoping the wire is cut, Robert leads his men carefully, across 'no man's land.'
i) We hear about Sergeant Smith's jokes and his story of the old woman.
j) They pull Morrison over the edge – but he dies anyway.
k) When they reach the enemy trench, a confused attack happens.
l) Finding nothing, Robert decides to lead the men back to the trench again.
m) Hearing that Morrison is missing, they go back out to the craters.
n) After the raid, they wriggle back to their own trench.
o) Robert shivers with horror, thinking back to the raid and the rescue.

Use the grid below to arrange each sentence in order (from 1–15) so that the plot unfolds as it happens.

1	2	3	4	5	6	7	8	9	10	11	12	13	14	15

Answers

1	2	3	4	5	6	7	8	9	10	11	12	13	14	15
a	i	h	k	n	m	l	b	g	e	c	j	d	o	f

Questions

Now that you have them in the correct order, try dividing the sentences up into the following categories. Which ones:

1. create an effective opening?
2. build tension towards the climax?
3. create a climax (usually near the end)?
4. resolve or 'round up' the story?
5. develop characters?
6. develop themes/ideas in the story? This might be tricky!

Remember that the same part of the plot might do more than one thing, for example:

e) Robert finds Morrison – and is shocked by the horrifying sight of him. This helps to build suspense, but also tells us something about Robert's character.

Why is it important that you know the story so well?

In the exam, you will be given an extract from a story. You need to be able to recognise where in the story your extract comes from and how it relates to the rest of the story.

It is also important to understand why Crichton Smith structured the plot in this way. You might notice that the events of the story help to build up suspense. For example, the soldiers get back to the trenches after the raid – and then notice that Morrison is missing. They go back out into no man's land and search for him – and then are back at their own trench again when they hear his cry for help. Back they go again – their third time in no man's land. And it is in the third (and last) crater that they finally find Morrison. All these delays in finding him – and each time they go out into danger again – help to build up the tension. Will they find him? Will more of them be killed in the search?

Now that you know the plot confidently, it's time to move on …

Characters

A short story usually has a small number of characters, with other people perhaps appearing in one incident or included to help develop a theme. Here are the characters named or mentioned in the story:

- Lieutenant Robert Mackinnon
- Sergeant Smith
- The old lady in Sergeant Smith's story
- Fred Morrison

- Harris
- Ellis
- Wright
- German soldier reading a book

This is quite a long list for a short story! But let's look more closely.

Task

Make a list of the characters and, beside each name, indicate:

- Which characters appear throughout the story?
- Which ones appear in only one part?
- Which ones could the story not exist without? (Imagine the story without character X – would it still make sense?)

You have probably found this is not as easy as it looks. For example, Morrison appears only towards the end of the story, but could the story really 'happen' without him? The attempt to rescue him is the climax of the story – so, he is important. But it's even more complicated – Morrison as a soldier to be rescued is important, but do we really get to know him as a personality? Compare what we learn about him and about Robert, for example.

Look again at your list of characters. Decide which ones are not really developed as full, rounded personalities and remove them from the list.

Hint!
Which of the characters can be 'summed up' in a word or phrase?

Your list has probably now been reduced to two: Robert and Sergeant Smith. The opening of the story introduces us to these two and Crichton Smith does something skilful with them straight away.

Read these quotations from the opening of the story:

1. 'He (Robert) kept thinking how similar it was to a play in which he had once taken part, and how the jokes before the performance had the same nervous high-pitched quality, as they prepared to go out into darkness.'

2. '… Smith himself had been invalided home and come back. "I missed your stink, lads," he had said when he appeared among them again, large and buoyant and happy.'

What is revealed here about Robert's and Sergeant Smith's different attitudes to the war?

We can see a **CONTRAST** in their attitudes to the war – and therefore, a **CONTRAST** in their personalities.

Task

Create a table with two headings like the one below. Decide which of the following descriptions matches each man – write down a list under each name.

Robert Mackinnon	Sergeant Smith

Which man is: imaginative? … matter of fact? … making the best of things? … sensitive? … apparently at home in the war situation? … struggling to make sense of it all? … has a relaxed relationship with the soldiers? … makes cheerful comments to put the men at ease? … quietly thinking his way through a tense situation?

Hint!
Some of the descriptions could be true of both men.

Which of the characters do we know better?

This is the character whose point of view we are given and invited to share throughout most of the story.

Hint!
Think about the names Crichton Smith uses for them.

Clearly, Robert is the main character of this story. Although he is an officer and in charge of the soldiers, he is inexperienced – this is his first raid – and we are invited to share his feelings of anxiety and uncertainty about the war and this raid in particular. Not only is he aware of the danger, but he also knows he has to establish himself as a leader – he has to earn the respect of the other men.

Task

Character study of Robert Mackinnon
We are going to get to know this central character a little better. Below is a list of quotations – and then a list of explanations. Try to match up each quotation with the best explanation in the grid below.

Quotations

1. 'He kept thinking how similar it all was to a play in which he had once taken part'
2. 'What am I doing here? thought Robert'
3. 'he had an idea of a huge mind breeding thought after thought, star after star'
4. 'This was his first raid and he thought, "I am frightened."'
5. 'he saw, or imagined he saw, a man inside reading a book'
6. 'We can't do anything till morning. He may be in one of the shallower ones.'
7. '"All right," he said. "We're going for him."'
8. 'He was about to say, "It's no good, he's dying," but something prevented him from saying it.'
9. 'This man must not fall down again into that lake. The death would be too terrible.'
10. 'Well, take him anyway. We're not leaving him here.'
11. 'What would Sergeant Smith think of him?'
12. 'This time we'll bloody well walk.'
13. 'he fell asleep … seeing page after page of comics set before him, like red windows, and in one there was a greenish monster'

Explanations

a) He relates the war to past experience to make sense of it all.
b) He is determined that Morrison will be saved from the horror of the crater.
c) After the horror of the crater, he takes a risk to assert human dignity.
d) He tries to avoid going back for Morrison if it is pointless.
e) He lacks experience – and knows it.
f) He cannot bring himself to tell the men their comrade will die.
g) He does not want to lose authority and respect in front of Smith.
h) He is haunted by the deaths of the enemy and his soldier.
i) He does not understand the war or his part in it.
j) He thinks imaginatively.
k) He makes a human connection, in his mind, with the enemy.
l) He realises that they must go back out to look for Morrison.
m) He wants to treat Morrison's body with the respect due to the man.

1	2	3	4	5	6	7	8	9	10	11	12	13

Answers

1	2	3	4	5	6	7	8	9	10	11	12	13
a	i	j	e	k	d	l	f	b	m	g	c	h

Theme

Now that you have a thorough grasp of the plot and characters of this story, we will look at how Crichton Smith uses both of these 'ingredients' to develop and convey a theme.

Task

We can see that war is a major theme of the story. What does Crichton Smith say to us about war, through his story and characters? Try bullet pointing three things he says to us about the nature of war in this story.

The most obvious thing is that he presents a NEGATIVE picture of war. It is not, in this story, about glory or heroism. War is seen as destructive and horrifying. It is also dehumanising, robbing people of their dignity as human beings. That does not mean, however, that no one is heroic in the story. Robert leads a rescue attempt in which he and the men risk their lives to try to save a comrade. That is heroic, even though Morrison dies. But the fact that he dies anyway – at the very moment they pull him out of the crater – makes us think: does heroism actually help anyone in a war situation? Robert shows compassion and respect for Morrison – both alive and dead – even though he is also horrified by the sight of him. But, do these feelings do any good? His action in walking (not crawling) back to the trench is a kind of defiance – asserting the dignity of humanity in the face of the horror of war. But does it achieve anything other than putting them all at risk? Sergeant Smith certainly feels that Robert almost got them killed, but he also seems to have appreciated the drama of the moment.

Developing your analysis skills

In this section, we will look at how you can use your knowledge and skill to analyse an extract from the story.

> **Remember** that the extract in your exam could come from anywhere in any of the stories. There is no point in trying to guess or predict which extract will be chosen. There is no point in 'learning' the most 'important' part of the story. There is no such thing as an 'unimportant' part of the story – after all, Crichton Smith wrote and included them all. Every paragraph in the story matters; they are all valid and all play their parts. **Any part could be picked**.

The aim of this book is to develop your knowledge and analytical skills so that you can approach any extract with confidence.

We are going to read and analyse the following extract from the story. Start by reading it and, as you read, ask yourself:

- Where does this extract come in the story?
- What is the 'heart' of this extract – in other words, what are the really important things about it?

And he stood up. There was no reason for crawling any more. The night was clear. And they would have to hurry. And the other two stood up as well when they saw him doing so. He couldn't leave a man to die in the pit of green slime. 'We'll run,' he said. And they ran to the first one and listened. They cried fiercely, 'Are you there?' But there was no answer. Then they seemed to hear it from the next one and they were at that one soon too, peering down into the green slime, illuminated by moonlight. But there was no answer. There was one left and they made for that one. They screamed again, in the sound of the shells, and they seemed to hear an answer. They heard what seemed to be a bubbling. 'Are you there?' said Robert, bending down and listening. 'Can you get over here?' They could hear splashing and deep below them breathing, frantic breathing as if someone was frightened to death. 'It's all right,' he said, 'if you come over here, I'll send my rifle down. You two hang on to me,' he said to the others. He was terrified. That depth, that green depth. Was Morrison down there, after all? He hadn't spoken. The splashings came closer. The voice was like an animal's repeating endlessly a mixture of curses and prayers. Robert hung over the edge of the crater.

Some ideas about this extract

This is the moment when they find Morrison in the crater. Notice the opening sentences (always a good idea!).

'And he stood up. There was no need for crawling any more.'

The words 'any more' suggest that they have been crawling previously. Immediately we might ask ourselves, why is there no need to crawl now? An answer is given when we are told they are trying to hurry – obviously running or walking will get them there more quickly than crawling. So we have the first sign of their urgency to find Morrison quickly.

The really important things about this extract – the 'heart' of the passage – involve the feelings of Robert and the men as they search for, find and try to rescue Morrison. These feelings can be divided up into four stages:

1. panic/urgency/desperate need to find him
2. uncertainty – they can't find him
3. Robert's fear – while trying to reassure Morrison that they will save him
4. Robert's doubt/terror – he is not even sure that it is Morrison down there.

Notice how Crichton Smith continues to develop the character of Robert and his relationship with the men. For example, when Robert stands up, we are told that the other two men do too. Also, '"We'll run," he said. And they ran …'. Notice that it is Robert who has the idea of using his rifle and Robert who hangs over the edge. What does all this show us about his place in the group and relationship with the other soldiers?

We can see that Robert, though inexperienced and scared, is leading the group. He has the ideas; he makes the decisions. The men follow his lead, which suggests that they respect him. Also, he is prepared to risk his own life – he does not order one of the other men to hang over the edge – which shows that he feels responsible for Morrison.

Techniques used in this extract

Read over the extract again and try to find one example of the each of the following techniques. How does each technique help to make this moment in the story dramatic? Remember that the thoughts and feelings of the men are very important in this extract.

word choice   dialogue   repetition   imagery   short sentences

Here is one example of each (you may have spotted different ones):

- word choice: 'fiercely' emphasises the sense of urgency as they desperately try to find him
- dialogue: 'Are you there? Can you get over here?' questions highlight their panic
- repetition: 'That depth, that green depth.' reinforces a sense of danger due to deep pools of slime
- imagery: 'like an animal's' emphasises intuitive, animal-like striving to survive, not reasoned, thoughtful, human response
- short sentences: 'He was terrified.' captures sudden moment of fear

Questions

National 5 exam-style questions

Now try to answer these questions on the extract. They are similar to the kind of questions you will face in the National 5 exam.

1. 'And he stood up.'
   Explain what the soldiers are doing at the start of this extract and why they were crawling before this moment. **(2 marks)**
2. Robert Mackinnon is in command of the rescue party. Give one example of a technique used by the writer to show that he is in command. **(2 marks)**
3. By referring to **two** examples of techniques used in the extract, show how suspense is built up. **(4 marks)**
4. Robert Mackinnon experiences horror but shows courage in this extract. Show how the writer conveys both his horror and courage, referring to **one** example of a technique used to show his horror and **one** example of a technique used to show his courage. **(4 marks)**

Possible answers

(Remember there may be many other correct answers.)

1. Attempting to rescue Morrison **(1 mark)**

   Danger of enemy fire **(1 mark)**

2. Dialogue: 'We'll run.' **(1 mark)**

   He decides for the whole group **(1 mark)**

   OR

   Description of actions: he stood up and others do so too **(1 mark)**

   Indicates that they look to him for guidance on what to do **(1 mark)**

3. Word choice: 'fiercely' **(1 mark)**

   Shows their panic/feeling of urgency **(1 mark)**

   Short sentence: 'But there was no answer.' **(1 mark)**

   Creates sense of drama/panic **(1 mark)**

4. **Horror:** repetition – 'That depth, that green depth.' **(1 mark)**

   Emphasises his feelings of fear/revulsion at huge pit of slime **(1 mark)**

   OR

   Simile – 'voice was like an animal's' **(1 mark)**

   Shows that Morrison's humanity has been replaced by raw, primitive suffering/instinct to survive **(1 mark)**

   Courage: word choice (or short sentence) – 'He was terrified.' **(1 mark)**

   Shows his extreme fear, yet he still goes ahead with rescue **(1 mark)**

   OR

   Dialogue – 'You two hold on to me.' **(1 mark)**

   Shows it is his decision to put himself at risk for Morrison **(1 mark)**

Questions

Higher exam-style questions

1. 'And he stood up.' Explain why this is a significant moment and analyse how the writer emphasises its significance. **(2 marks)**
2. Analyse how language is used to reveal Mackinnon's contrasting reactions to the discovery of Morrison. **(4 marks)**

Possible answers

1. Significant because Mackinnon asserts himself/shows his determination to rescue Morrison, no matter the danger **(1 mark)**

   Short sentence: dramatic/captures immediacy **(1 mark)**

   OR

   Beginning with 'And ...' emphasises sudden nature of decision **(1 mark)**

2. Horror conveyed by 'That depth, that green depth.' Repetition emphasises his awareness of the endless pit below and revulsion at the slime filling it **(up to 2 marks)**

   Determination to save Morrison conveyed by dialogue 'You two hang on to me.' Use of command emphasises Mackinnon's determination to find a practical solution, will save him at risk to self **(up to 2 marks)**

Marking scheme

- 0 marks for quotation/reference alone
- For full marks both sides of the contrast must be covered.
- 2 marks for detailed/insightful answer + quote/reference (x2 for 4)
- 1 mark for more basic answer + reference

Question

Looking ahead …

This is the sort of question you may meet as the final question:

5. Show how Crichton Smith develops the theme of conflict, by referring to this and at least one other short story you have studied.

At National 5 level, this sort of question is marked out of 8. At Higher, it is marked out of 10. Question 5, above, could appear as a National 5 or a Higher question, but a more sophisticated, developed answer would be expected at Higher level.

We will look at this in more detail later.

Now that you are an expert on 'The Crater', it is time to move on to another story.

'In Church'

From now on, you should read each story, not just individually for what you can 'get out of it' in terms of enjoyment and making you think, but comparatively – in other words, thinking about how it compares with the other stories you have read by Crichton Smith. Remember that these six stories have all been chosen for a reason – there are links between them, perhaps in terms of plot, characters, setting and/or theme. You will spot similarities and also differences. This makes for exciting reading, keeping us intrigued. It is also something we will return to later, when looking at the final, 'big mark' question.

Read the story 'In Church' and note down any three similarities and three differences between this story and 'The Crater'. To start you off, they are both set in wartime, so we would expect some similarities. On the other hand, they are not both set on the front line of the battlefield, so we might expect some differences.

Answers

Similarities (both stories)
set in wartime
involve a sense of danger or threat
show how destructive war is
involve a main character – young soldier – decent, thoughtful person
build to a climax
involve a death
suggest heartlessness of the authorities
suggest that surviving war as a sensitive person is difficult
suggest that being a good person will not save you

Differences	
'The Crater'	'In Church'
set on front line	set in a place of apparent safety
involves small group of soldiers on a raid	involves one soldier in conflict
death of less important character	death of main character
attempt to save Morrison's life	MacLeod deliberately murdered
war destroys by killing	war also destroys by dehumanising people
a military raid	murder by deserter
we don't see Morrison's actual killer	priest/deserter important character
suggests survival is possible (e.g. Smith)	no way out of death/suffering

Plot

The plot of this story is deceptively simple: much of the narrative impact comes from the build up of suspense as MacLeod becomes increasingly uneasy after he meets the 'priest'. To make sure you understand how this works, note down a quick list of five things that happen in the story. Beside each one, identify how MacLeod is feeling at that point in the story.

Possible answers

What happens	How MacLeod feels
He watches the birds fighting overhead.	Sickened – can't stand to watch any more
He enters the church.	Awkward – style of church is unfamiliar
The priest speaks to him in English.	Astonished – it is like a nightmare
He is taken to the priest's underground 'lair' in the crypt.	Uneasy and horrified by bones, blood, etc.
Priest tells him to sit and listen to 'sermon'.	He is in a 'dream', with no power to resist

Questions

Now, some questions to get you thinking. You might tackle these as a group and compare ideas. There may be many different ideas, all of them valid.

1. At what point did you feel MacLeod was in danger?
2. When did you begin to suspect that the priest was not a real priest?
3. Was the ending a shock? Why/why not?
4. MacLeod's death is ironic in various ways. Can you spot any of the ironic aspects?

Knowing the characters confidently

There are only two characters, MacLeod and the priest, so each one is very important. At a first glance, they might seem like opposites – murderer and victim – one a decent, loyal soldier, the other a deranged killer. However, as this is a brilliantly written story, it is not as simple as this.

Questions

Answer these questions on the two characters. Which of them:

1. had more positive life prospects before the war?
2. has lost his sense of what it is to be a decent human being?
3. is trying to hold on to a feeling of justice and fairness?
4. is a victim of the war?
5. does not have a positive future?
6. questions the point of the war?
7. is angry and frustrated by the violence?
8. is out of place in the church?

We can see that, in many cases, the two men are similar. This is not just a story about an encounter between a 'goody' and a 'baddy'. In a way, the priest could almost be a 'version' of MacLeod, if he had not been killed, but lived through more horrors. What is Crichton Smith suggesting about the effects of war on people? If we do see MacLeod as the hero of the story and the deserter as the villain, then Crichton Smith is presenting us with a bleak picture of what can happen to decent, heroic types in war. In a way, the random nature of the death makes this point all the more forcefully: MacLeod's death is pointless, killed by one of his own side – and by someone who shares his feelings about the war. It achieves nothing.

Developing your analysis skills

Let's take a closer look at the priest/deserter character, who provides most of the tension and mystery in the story. Here is the moment when MacLeod first meets him. As you read this part again, think about how Crichton Smith is using language to build up a picture of this man. Remember that the church appears abandoned, so the sudden appearance of the priest is surprising in itself.

> He could feel in his bones the presence of past generations of worshippers, and then he heard the footsteps.
>
> He turned round to see a man in a black gown walking towards him. There was a belt of rope round his gown and his hands could not be seen as they seemed to be folded inside his gown. The face was pale and ill looking.
>
> 'What do you want, my son?' said the voice in English.

Question

What does Crichton Smith achieve in this moment?

It is not simply the arrival of another character. Note down any significant examples of language used to create an impression of the 'priest'.

Possible answers

- Notice that the first 'warning' MacLeod has of the priest's approach is the sound of his footsteps. And Crichton Smith calls them '**the** footsteps', suggesting that this sound is significant. Someone important is coming.
- MacLeod 'turned round to see' – the priest seems to be almost creeping up behind MacLeod. He does not speak until up close.
- The priest's gown is mentioned several times. MacLeod sees 'a man in a black gown ... rope round his gown' and 'his hands could not be seen as they seemed to be folded inside his gown.' Why is there such emphasis on the gown? A roomy garment with folds of material, it gives a certain mystery to the character and is more noticeable than the man itself. Who – or what – is inside the gown? MacLeod, at first, is not sure.
- 'The face was pale and ill looking'. Why 'the face' instead of 'his face'? This makes the priest seem less human, more like a ghostly presence – and of course 'pale' and 'ill looking' add to this.
- After all that, the kindly words 'What do you want, my son?' are surprising. Maybe he is just a nice man after all? But already we are just a bit suspicious of him – and perhaps MacLeod is too?
- Final point – why does he speak in English? Another mystery – maybe he recognises MacLeod's uniform? Or (as it turns out) could he be British himself?

See how such an apparently simple moment in the story can suggest so much.

Now, we will analyse a later moment, when the 'priest' has taken MacLeod down into the crypt. Watch out for use of dialogue this time!

All over the floor, bones were scattered, and there seemed to be an assortment of bloody animal traps.

'Rabbit bones,' said the priest smiling. 'Bones of hares. It is not very …'

'You mean you …'

'This is how I live,' said the priest. 'I have no bread to offer you, I'm afraid. If you would please sit down?'

'I think I had better …'

'I said please sit down. I shall tell you about myself. I have lived now for a year by myself. Alone. What do you think of that?' The priest smiled, showing blackened teeth.

At this point MacLeod is feeling quite uneasy. Show how the details given below contribute to his feeling of uneasiness.

1. Bones over the floor
2. Bloody traps
3. 'Rabbit bones'
4. 'the priest smiled'
5. 'This is how I live … I have no bread to offer you …'
6. 'I said please sit down'
7. 'I have lived now for a year by myself. Alone.'
8. 'blackened teeth'

Possible answers

Points 1, 2, 3 and 8 convey the primitive, almost animal existence of the priest, while points 5 and 7 suggest that he has accepted this lonely, not quite human life. But why would someone choose to live like this?

Point 4 makes him seem sinister and peculiar – not a warm, comforting smile in the context.

In point 6 he is commanding MacLeod, dominating him (with still the façade of politeness).

And finally …

The priest delivers a sermon to a congregation of one, MacLeod. By this time MacLeod knows he is with someone whose mind is not working normally. How does he react? He obeys, sits down feeling 'as if he were in a dream'.

He also knows he is the priest's prisoner: how do we know? The priest says, 'I shall not pray because that would mean closing my eyes … you might run away.'

What the priest says in his sermon is another surprise: his story of how he came to be living like an animal in the middle of the war. This is a long speech – the longest in the story. What is Crichton Smith's purpose in including it? Let's examine some 'clips'.

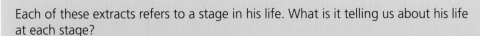

Each of these extracts refers to a stage in his life. What is it telling us about his life at each stage?

- 'I grew up innocent and hopeful.'
- 'At … eighteen I was forced into the army to fight for what they call one's country.'
- 'I was put among men whom I despised and feared … Yet they were my comrades'
- 'I was being shot at by strangers'
- 'One day I could bear no more of the killing'

Look again at the final quotation: 'One day I could bear no more of the killing'. Doesn't this sound very like, 'He couldn't stand watching the fight any more'? – said about MacLeod, the soldier who has *not* deserted.

Perhaps Crichton Smith is suggesting that they are not so different after all.

None of the comments made by the 'priest' seem like the words of a killer. It is his experience of the war itself – and his fear that he will be caught and sent back (or shot as a deserter) – that makes him kill. Ultimately, he is angry with God for allowing the war to happen.

Now look at these quotations, taken from later in the deserter's life story.
Can you explain what each tells us about his developing character?

- 'Lord you have cheated me. You in your immense absence.'
- 'I have lived like an animal.'
- 'I hate you because you have not intervened to save the world.'

As the 'priest' finishes his sermon, MacLeod agrees with him. They have, potentially, a connection BUT the 'priest' believes that, as a soldier – and an officer – MacLeod will do his duty and hand him in to the authorities. So war (in this case, MacLeod's military responsibility) destroys any chance for human understanding and connection. And the deserter is so sure that MacLeod will report him, that he shoots him.

Theme

Clearly the main theme of this story is war – and, again, Crichton Smith is showing us how destructive it is. We can see, from the activities above, that plot and characters are used to develop the theme. Let's look at other features used to say something about war.

Setting

Most of the story takes place inside the church: the title of the story shows how important this setting is. This should be a place of peace and safety – in fact, both the characters have ended up in the church seeking peace. True, the deserter has been there long term, surviving by hiding in the crypt and disguising himself as a priest. But MacLeod also had the urge to seek safety and calm within the church. As we see, war means that death lurks in apparently safe places.

Opening

The story begins with Lieutenant MacLeod feeling 'released for a short while from the war'. He is behind the front lines (unlike the soldiers in 'The Crater'); looking up at the 'pale blue sky' he waves to a pilot (an ally) and the gunfire is 'faint'. It seems almost pleasant …

Now read the following quotations. Decide how each quotation helps to create a picture of normality.

- 'one could begin to use one's ears again'
- 'smoke rising in the far distance seemed to belong to another war'
- 'how unreal a battle might become'

Suddenly, this peaceful atmosphere is interrupted by images of death.

Complete these images of death and destruction.

1. During a previous attack, the trenches were full of _____.
2. What could hit the soldiers at any time?
3. What had been 'worked over and over'?
4. What were birds doing in the sky above?
5. The German pilot in a previous fight appears _____ but is _____.

Possible answers

1. Dead bodies
2. Death/artillery shells (from the distance)
3. The 'scarred ground'
4. Two birds attacking a third
5. Alive ('upright, disciplined, aristocratic')/dead

These images of death foreshadow the death that is to come, ironically, in such a peaceful place.

'The Telegram'

Quick info quest

Make sure you know what a 'telegram' is and who an 'elder' is.

This is one of Iain Crichton Smith's best-known and best-loved stories. It delivers a strong anti-war message, but this time not by describing conflict on the battlefield or murder behind the lines. Let's see how it's done.

Setting
Plot
Characters
Theme

Setting and plot

Again, the setting is in wartime, but Crichton Smith shifts the focus away from the battle scene altogether – to back home, where the parents of soldiers wait anxiously for news. It is set in a small community: one street; one house; a kitchen; two women sitting at a window. The plot is extremely simple. The two women watch the village elder walking up the street towards their houses, wondering which house will receive the dreaded telegram. The elder walks past into the countryside: the telegram was about his own son.

Question

What is the effect of setting a war story here, far away from the actual fighting? How does Crichton Smith build up tension in this simple plot?

Possible answer

Crichton Smith shows how devastating war is, not just for the soldiers, but for their families back home. For these people, the war is just as real and terrible.

Tension is built up in 'The Telegram' by the effectively simple plot device of the elder walking along the street, while the two mothers watch him approach. With each house he passes, the chances increase of it being one of the two women's sons who has died. As they wait and watch, we share their thoughts and comments – often about each other, their sons and village life. This helps to build tension towards the emotional climax, as each woman thinks she has lost her only son.

Characters

The two women, mothers with sons at war, are the main characters. It's worth noting that, apart from one part near the end when one calls the other 'Sarah', they are not given names at all – apart from the unflattering descriptions 'fat woman' and 'thin woman'. Why do you think Crichton Smith chose to do this?

Task

A closer look at characters

Here are some quotations from the story. Decide which woman each is referring to or which woman said what – and what is being suggested about her. The first two are quite easy.

1. 'a fat domestic bird'
2. 'more aquiline, more gaunt … more like a buzzard'
3. 'not popular in the village'
4. 'when he comes home on leave he's never in the house. But I don't mind.'
5. 'she had sent her son to university, though she only had a widow's pension!'
6. 'he might not give me anything after all I've done for him'
7. 'her own child … whom she had seen running home from school'

These final ones are thought **by** the 'fat woman' **about** the 'thin woman'. What do they suggest about each woman?

8. 'you couldn't feel at ease with her, you had the idea all the time that she was thinking about something else'
9. 'she sipped her tea, her little finger elegantly curled in an irritating way'
10. 'it was like first love … such an innocent gesture'
11. 'Where did she learn that self-control?'

Possible answers

Points 1, 4, 7: the 'fat woman' is basically a contented, unimaginative person. She accepts that her son will neglect her (that's what a man 'should' do). At the moment of crisis though, she is haunted by a memory of him as a little boy.

Points 2, 3, 5, 6: the 'thin woman' is a hardworking, self-denying person, not accepted by the community as they see her attempts to educate her son as 'getting above herself'. Ironically, she realises that sending him to university might mean that he leaves her behind when he climbs socially.

Points 8 and 9 show the 'fat woman's' dislike of the 'thin woman': she sees her as distant and snobbish.

Point 10 is the moment when she feels comforted by her.

Point 11 she admires her for being able to cope with (supposed) tragedy so well.

Linking setting and characters to theme

Task

Look again at point 3 in the task above and read the quotations below. This time, work out what Crichton Smith is saying about the small community environment – an important theme in his work.

1. 'She was an incomer from another village and had only been in this one for thirty years or so.'
2. 'She didn't want to cry in front of that woman. That foreigner'
3. 'Did you hear … that Malcolm MacKay was up on a drunken charge?'
4. '"They say his wife had one of her fits again," said the fat woman viciously.'

Possible answers

Points 1 and 2 show that the thin woman is not accepted after 'only'(!) thirty years of living in the village. She is still a 'foreigner'. Crichton Smith is indicating the extremely parochial and small-minded attitudes of village folk. He suggests their enjoyment of malicious gossip and judgemental comments in points 3 and 4. Not a very positive picture of village life!

Now it's time to try an exam-style activity. Read the extract below and answer the questions that follow.

'The Telegram'

And at that moment the fat woman saw. She saw the years of discipline, she remembered how thin and unfed and pale the thin woman had always looked, how sometimes she had had to borrow money, even a shilling to buy food. She saw what it must have been like to be a widow bringing up a son in a village not her own. She saw it so clearly that she was
5   astounded. It was as if she had an extra vision, as if the air itself brought the past with all its details nearer. The number of times the thin woman had been ill and people had said that she was weak and useless. She looked down at the thin woman's arm. It was so shrivelled and dry.

And the elder walked on. A few yards now till he reached the plank. But the thin woman
10 hadn't cried. She was steady and still, her lips still compressed, sitting upright in her chair. And, miracle of miracles, the elder missed the plank and walked straight on.

They looked at each other. What did it all mean? Where was the elder going, clutching his telegram in his hand, walking like a man in a daze? There were no other houses so where was he going? They drank their tea in silence, turning away from each other. The fat woman
15 said, 'I must be going.' They parted for the moment without speaking. The thin woman still sat at the window looking out.

Once or twice the fat woman made as if to turn back as if she had something to say, some message to pass on, but she didn't. She walked away.

It wasn't until later that night they discovered what had happened. The elder had a telegram
20 directed to himself, to tell him of the drowning of his own son. He should never have seen it just like that, but there had been a mistake at the post office, owing to the fact that there were two boys in the village with the same name. His walk through the village was a somnambulist wandering. He didn't want to go home and tell his wife what had happened. He was walking along not knowing where he was going when later he was stopped half way to the next village.
25 Perhaps he was going in search of his son. Altogether he had walked six miles. The telegram was crushed in his fingers and so sweaty that they could hardly make out the writing.

Questions

National 5 exam-style questions

1. 'And at that moment the fat woman saw.'
    a) Look closely at lines 1–8.
        Summarise in your own words what the fat woman 'saw' (i.e. understood) about the thin woman. **(2 marks)**
    b) By referring to one example, show how the writer uses language to emphasise aspects of the thin woman's life. **(2 marks)**
2. 'the thin woman hadn't cried'
    Look at lines 9–11.
    By referring to one example, show how the writer uses word choice to emphasise the thin woman's self-control. **(2 marks)**
3. Look at lines 12–18.
    By referring to one example, show how the writer's use of language emphasises the feelings of the women. **(2 marks)**
4. Look at lines 19–26. Here are two alternative questions on this part.
    By referring to two examples of word choice, show how the writer emphasises the effect the telegram had on the elder. **(4 marks)**
    OR
    (line 19) '… they discovered what had happened.'
    In your own words, explain what had happened to the elder. **(4 marks)**

Final question

5. Show how Iain Crichton Smith develops the theme of conflict in this and at least one other short story. **(8 marks)**

Possible answers

1. **a)** Thin woman endured hardship/poverty/hunger/loneliness – no husband/isolation in village/ criticism from neighbours **(any two for 1 mark + 1 mark)**
    b) Possible examples include: 'thin and unfed' emphasises poverty – literally giving up her food for sake of her son; 'pale … thin' suggests unwell, never getting chance to be healthy due to hard life; 'weak and useless' – lack of compassion in others' judgements of her; 'shrivelled' suggests youth gone, close to death …
    1 mark for example; 1 mark for explanation

2. Possible examples include: 'steady and still' suggests calm, preventing herself from moving/fidgeting; 'lips still compressed' – feelings being kept in, mouth shut tight to prevent outburst of feeling; 'sitting upright' suggests firmness, determination to behave 'properly' …
    1 mark for example; 1 mark for explanation

3. Possible examples include: (repeated) use of questions suggests confusion; word choice 'silence'/'without speaking' – don't know what to say to each other; brief expression 'but she didn't' suggests awkwardness/moment of closeness is over
    1 mark for example; 1 mark for explanation

4. Here are the two alternative marking instructions.
    Possible answers include: 'somnambulist wandering' emphasises the daze he is in, as if asleep; repetition of 'He …' reinforces sense of his own suffering; 'crushed' suggests anguish while holding telegram; 'sweaty' suggests extreme emotion felt while holding telegram
    1 mark for example; 1 mark for explanation (x2)

OR

He had seen telegram about death of own son/due to mix up of telegrams

Shocked/dazed/couldn't face wife/walking aimlessly ... other answers possible

1 mark for each point (x4)

5. Theme of conflict **(total = 8 marks)**

Identifying 'commonality' **(up to 2 marks)**:

- Crichton Smith presents the conflict of war as a completely devastating force/often not understood by those it affects/not about glory or heroes winning.

Referring to extract **(up to 2 marks)**:

- In extract, we see the pain of parents back home (two women and elder) waiting for news of their sons far away at war.

Possible references to other texts **(up to 4 marks)**:

- 'The Crater' – soldier Morrison becomes 'monstrous' due to slime in crater he falls into – horrifies Mackinnon, his rescuer.
- 'In Church' – deserter turned priest also a 'monster' – fear of war has driven him to live like an animal and commit murder.
- Mackinnon shows heroism and compassion in trying to rescue Morrison but it is pointless – he dies anyway.

Questions

Higher exam-style questions

1. 'And at that moment the fat woman saw.'
   a) Explain the contrast between the fat woman's new 'view' of the thin woman and the opinion previously held by the community. **(2 marks)**
   b) Analyse how language is used to convey her new view of the thin woman. **(2 marks)**

2. 'It wasn't until later that night they discovered what had happened.'
   a) Explain the irony of what had happened. **(2 marks)**
   b) Show how language is used to convey the impact of what had happened on the elder. **(4 marks)**

Final question

3. Show how Iain Crichton Smith develops the theme of conflict in this and at least one other short story. **(10 marks)**

(This question would be suitable for both National 5 and Higher. The standard of answer will be different at Higher.)

Possible answers

1. a) New: her self-sacrificing/isolated/heroic struggle **(1 mark)**
   Previous: she was physically pathetic/had no drive or determination **(1 mark)**
   b) 'thin and unfed': sense of her sacrifice, literally giving her son all her food;
   'pale and thin': suggests unhealthy, lacking in life or rich enjoyment;
   'shrivelled and dry': suggests ageing, near death, no sense of life or promise of the future

   (2 marks for detailed/insightful comment + reference; 1 mark for more basic comment + reference; 0 marks for reference alone)

2. a) It was his son who had died/neither of them had actually lost their son. **(1 mark)**
Although they spent the whole story wondering which one of them it was/although the elder was usually the bringer of bad news to others **(1 mark)**

b) Repetitive opening focusing on him: 'He should never … His walk … He didn't …' indicates relentless nature of the shock for him.

OR

Word choice: 'crushed'/'sweaty' emphasises the physical expression of his extreme anguish.

(2 marks for detailed/insightful comment + reference; 1 mark for more basic comment + reference; 0 marks for reference alone)

Final question marking scheme at Higher level

Up to 2 marks can be achieved for identifying elements of commonality as identified in the question, i.e. the destructive nature of conflict. A further 2 marks can be achieved for reference to the extract given. 6 additional marks can be awarded for discussion of similar references to at least one other short story by Crichton Smith.

In practice this means:

- Identification of commonality **(up to 2 marks)** – theme of conflict. A general comment on how Crichton Smith develops the theme of conflict
  E.g. Conflict in war destroys the humanity in people as well as killing them physically. However, people do sometimes show heroism and compassion in times of conflict **(2 marks)**

From the extract:

- **Up to 2 marks** for comment on the theme of conflict in this extract
  E.g. Agony felt by the elder shown in the 'crushed' telegram and his inability to face the truth of his own loss through conflict – although he frequently tells others of their tragedies **(2 marks)**

From at least one other text:

- As above (x3) for up to 6 marks

OR

- More detailed comment (x2) for up to 6 marks

Thus, the final 6 marks can be gained by a combination of 3, 2 and 1 marks, depending on the level of depth/detail/insight. The aim would be to encourage quality of comment, rather than quantity of references.

Possible answers include:

- 'The Crater': the raid is an 'insignificant' conflict in the eyes of the authorities but still causes horrific suffering and death **(2 marks)**
- 'The Crater': Morrison turning into a 'monster' in the green slime symbolises what the conflict of war does to humanity **(2 marks)**
- 'In Church': the deserter/priest is dehumanised by his experience of conflict and has neither human dignity nor compassion, killing MacLeod to survive **(2 marks)**

'Mother and Son'

Setting, plot and characters

The setting, just as in 'The Telegram' is in a small community – but even 'smaller'. John and his mother live on a small farm – a croft – outside the village; the story is set in the one room which functions as their kitchen, living room and bedroom for the old lady. There is very little space and the story has a claustrophobic feeling – which reflects John's life. He, too, is trapped. The plot is very simple: it describes an evening in the life of John, after he comes in from working on the croft. The tension is built up this time through the relationship between John and his mother. While he goes about the practical business of caring for his mother, she responds with accusations and criticisms. His frustration grows – and he approaches the bed in the climax of the story.

Plot and character analysis

Task

A. Choose three things that John does for his mother in the course of the evening.

B. Match up these remarks, made by John's mother, with the explanations below.

1. 'It's only you.'
2. 'My father was never like you. He was a man who knew his business.'
3. 'Do you know what's going to happen to you, you'll be taken to the asylum.'
4. 'Of course Roddy doesn't want to help you.'
5. 'Why, you'd be no good in a job … The manager would always be coming to show you what you'd done wrong … They'd laugh at you.'
6. 'Why didn't you wash this tray? Can't you see it's all dirty round the edges?'
7. 'Cigarettes again? Don't you know that there's very little money coming into the house?'

→

Explanations

a) She accuses him of wasting money.
b) She questions his sanity.
c) She is disappointed when he comes home.
d) She undermines his confidence about working beyond the croft.
e) He will never live up to her own family's achievements.
f) When he is helping her, she always finds something to complain about.
g) She sides with those who do not want to assist him.

1	2	3	4	5	6	7

C. Now, let's look at John's frustration, which builds up through (A) and (B).
Again, match up each quotation with an explanation below.

1. 'He sat staring into the fire and answered dully, "Yes, it's only me."'
2. '"All right, all right," he said despairingly. "Can't you get a new record for your gramophone."'
3. 'He moved about inside this sea of sound trying to keep detached, trying to force himself from listening.'
4. 'Most often however they [her criticisms] stung him and stood quivering in his flesh.'
5. '… she would strike his confidence dead with her hateful words'
6. '… he felt himself in a dark cave from which there was never to be any escape'
7. '… a rage shook him, so great that he flung his half-consumed cigarette … in an abrupt, savage gesture'
8. 'How he hated her!'
9. 'He would show her, avenge her insults with his unintelligent hands.'

Explanations

a) Her comments destroy his self-esteem.
b) He accepts his own insignificance.
c) Defiance and revenge at last!
d) He feels he is trapped forever.
e) He tries to stop her from repeating the same criticisms.
f) Her comments cause him terrible pain.
g) He realises how far from a loving relationship they have come.
h) He tries to ignore the overwhelming flood of criticism hitting him.
i) An outburst of anger, beginning to show itself in physical action.

1	2	3	4	5	6	7	8	9

Answers

A. Lights the lamp, lights the fire, makes her tea (to drink), makes her supper, provides companionship.

B.

1	2	3	4	5	6	7
c	e	b	g	d	f	a

C.

1	2	3	4	5	6	7	8	9
b	e	h	f	a	d	i	g	c

Climax

John's resentment, rage and feeling of being trapped has built up. In the final moments of the story, he is advancing on the bed, intending to take violent revenge on his mother, for all the insults that have destroyed his confidence and trapped him at home.

What happens next? Why does this happen? What sort of feeling are we left with at the end?

Possible answer

His mother is asleep and he does not, after all, attack her with his 'unintelligent hands'. She is lying there, totally defenceless and vulnerable – so maybe he feels sorry for her? But Crichton Smith is very unsentimental – this is no 'Hollywood movie' ending when they hug and make up. The smile on her face as she sleeps is 'bitter, bitter' and he stands looking at her with 'an equally bitter smile curled up at the edge of his lips'. He does not suddenly realise how much he loves her: it's more an acceptance that he cannot and will not harm her. Then he walks to the door, opens it – but does not escape into the world. He just stands in the doorway, listening to the rain, still trapped. The feeling at the end is depressing: there is no way out for John.

Read this extract and answer the questions that follow.

'Mother and Son'

He turned round on his chair from a sudden impulse and looked at her intensely. He had
done this very often before, had tried to cow her into submission: but she had always
laughed at him. Now however he was looking at her as if he had never seen her before. Her
mouth was open and there were little crumbs upon her lower lip. Her face had sharpened
5 itself into a birdlike quickness: she seemed to be pecking at the bread with a sharp beak in
the same way as she pecked cruelly at his defences. He found himself considering her as if
she were some kind of animal. Detachedly he thought: how can this thing make my life a
hell for me? What is she anyway? She's been ill for ten years: that doesn't excuse her. She's
breaking me up so that even if she dies I won't be any good for anyone. But what if she's
10 pretending? What if there is nothing wrong with her? At this a rage shook him so great that
he flung his half-consumed cigarette in the direction of the fire in an abrupt, savage gesture.
Out of the silence he heard a bus roaring past the window, splashing over the puddles. That
would be the boys going to the town to enjoy themselves. He shivered inside his loneliness
and then rage took hold of him again. How he hated her! This time his gaze concentrated
15 itself on her scraggy neck, rising like a hen's out of her plain white nightgown. He watched
her chin wagging up and down: it was stained with jam and flecked with one or two
crumbs. His sense of loneliness closed around him, so that he felt as if he were on a boat
on the limitless ocean, just as his house was on a limitless moorland. There was a calm,
unspeaking silence, while the rain beat like a benediction on the roof. He walked over to the
20 bed, took the tray from her as she held it out to him. He had gone in answer to words which
he hadn't heard, so hedged was he in his own thoughts.

Questions

National 5 exam-style questions

1. 'He had done this very often before …'
   Explain in your own words what he had done before and how effective it had been. **(2 marks)**

2. Crichton Smith uses the following images to convey John's view of his mother: lines 4–6,
   'Her face had sharpened … at his defences' and lines 14–16, 'This time his gaze … nightgown.'
   Pick one of these images and analyse its effectiveness in showing John's feelings towards
   his mother. **(2 marks)**

3. Look at lines 6–10, 'He found himself … wrong with her?' By referring to two examples,
   show how language is used to show John's reaction to his mother. **(4 marks)**

4. Explain how the sound of the bus going past (line 12) adds to John's negative feelings. **(2 marks)**

5. '… he felt as if he were on a boat on the limitless ocean …' Explain fully what this image
   suggests about John's life. **(2 marks)**

Final question

6. In his stories, Crichton Smith often creates characters that feel – or are – trapped in a situation.
   By referring to this and at least one other story by Crichton Smith, show how he does this. **(8 marks)**

Possible answers

1. Stared at her/tried to dominate her **(1 mark)**

   Did not work/she mocked him **(1 mark)**

2. 'Her face … defences': image of bird attacking him like prey/food **(1 mark)**

   Effectively suggests her sharpness/vicious comments/lack of compassion **(1 mark)**

   OR

   'This time … nightgown': image of hen with scraggy neck/ugliness/not human **(1 mark)**

   Suggests his revulsion/no longer seeing her as human (due to cruel treatment) **(1 mark)**

3. Examples include:

   'some kind of animal' **(1 mark)**; lack of human/maternal warmth **(1 mark)**

   'this thing' **(1 mark)**; does not see her as human due to her cruelty **(1 mark)**

   Repeated use of questions **(1 mark)**; he is questioning his acceptance of her so far/his life and its meaning **(1 mark)**

   'breaking me up' **(1 mark)**; violent language suggests how destructive her treatment of him is **(1 mark)**

4. Other young men heading into town/enjoying themselves **(1 mark)**

   Adds to his sense of his own misery/feeling trapped **(1 mark)**

5. Alone **(1 mark)**

   Distant from others **(1 mark)**

6. Commonality – **up to 2 marks**, e.g. stories show characters can be trapped by external circumstances (such as war) and by relationships

   Up to 2 marks for 'Mother and Son': e.g. John's confidence undermined by constant criticism + reference/quote

   Up to 4 marks for other stories, e.g. 'In Church': MacLeod trapped by deserter/deserter also trapped by dehumanising effects of war + reference/quote

   'The Crater': Morrison is trapped in crater (represents horror of war)/Mackinnon – decent/sensitive person trapped in war + reference/quote

   'The Telegram': women trapped waiting for news of their sons + reference/quote

Questions

Higher exam-style questions

Look at lines 6–10 ('He found himself … wrong with her?').

1. Explain how John's thoughts about his relationship with his mother develop in this section. **(2 marks)**
2. Analyse how language is used to convey his thoughts and/or feelings in this section. **(4 marks)**

Final question

3. In his stories, Crichton Smith often creates characters that feel – or are – trapped in the situation they are in. By referring to this and at least one other story by Crichton Smith, show how he does this. **(10 marks)**

(This question would be suitable for both National 5 and Higher. The standard of answer will be different at Higher.)

Possible answers

1. Distancing himself from her/realisation of the damage she has done to him **(1 mark)**; begins wondering if she has deliberately deceived him into looking after her/anger at this possibility **(1 mark)**

2. Word choice, e.g. 'Detachedly', 'this thing' emphasises that he is not thinking of her as his mother but as an inhuman external force acting on him/emphasises his feelings of distance from her

   Metaphor 'breaking me up' emphasises scale of destruction she has caused to his confidence/personality

   Repeated use of questions suggests build up of frustration as he realises he may have been tricked

   2 marks (x2 for 4 marks) for detailed/insightful comment + reference; 1 mark for more basic comment + reference; 0 marks for reference alone **(4 marks)**

3. • **Up to 2 marks** can be achieved for identifying elements of commonality as identified in the question, i.e. characters who feel trapped in a situation
   • A further **2 marks** can be achieved for reference to the extract given
   • **6 additional marks** can be awarded for discussion of similar references to at least one other short story by the Crichton Smith.

In practice this means:

• Identification of commonality **(up to 2 marks)** – trapped characters
  E.g. Crichton Smith creates situations in which his characters are trapped, either by external circumstances, such as war, or by a destructive relationship **(2 marks)**

From the extract:

• **Up to 2 marks** for comment on trapped characters in this story
  E.g. John's confidence is so low (due to years of criticism by his mother) that he is unable to break away and even get a job beyond their croft, never mind leave her **(2 marks)**

From at least one other text:

• As above (x3) for **up to 6 marks**

OR

• More detailed comment (x2) for **up to 6 marks**

Thus, the final 6 marks can be gained by a combination of 3, 2 and 1 marks, depending on the level of depth/detail/insight. The aim would be to encourage quality of comment, rather than quantity of references.

In comments on other texts, possible references include:

• 'In Church': MacLeod trapped by deserter/deserter also trapped by dehumanising effects of war
• 'The Crater': Morrison is trapped in crater (represents horror of war)/Mackinnon – decent/sensitive person trapped in war
• 'The Telegram': women trapped waiting for news of their sons can only sit helplessly, watching death (in figure of elder) approaching them.

'The Painter'

In this story we again see setting, plot and character intertwined to develop theme. We find ourselves in a familiar small community similar to those from 'The Telegram' and 'Mother and Son'. This time the individual struggling against the 'trap' of community life is a highly creative person, an individual: the 'painter' of the title. However, there is a new aspect: the use of first person narrative. (This is the only one of our stories told in this way.) The story is told by one of the villagers, who is remembering events in his village from long ago.

Task

Consider the narrator. What is gained by having the story told in this way? Why is the narrator not given an actual name? What impression do you form of his personality?

Possible answer

First person narrative allows the writer to present the events of the story from a particular viewpoint and, therefore, to reveal the opinions – and prejudices – of the narrator. The narrator in 'The Painter' is unreliable – meaning that he lets his prejudices get in the way of a fair and honest version of events and characters. We see this in the way he describes William Murray, the painter – and in the climax of the story. By not giving him a name, Crichton Smith enables him to 'stand for' village opinion in general. We sense that he represents the view of the village – and his personality, small-minded and fiercely defensive, contributes to the climax, when he destroys William's creative effort rather than face an uncomfortable truth about his village, and himself.

Much of the story is not about the painter at all, but about another village 'character', Red Roderick. To understand what Crichton Smith is saying about the theme of individuality versus conformity, let's look at these two personalities and their roles in the village.

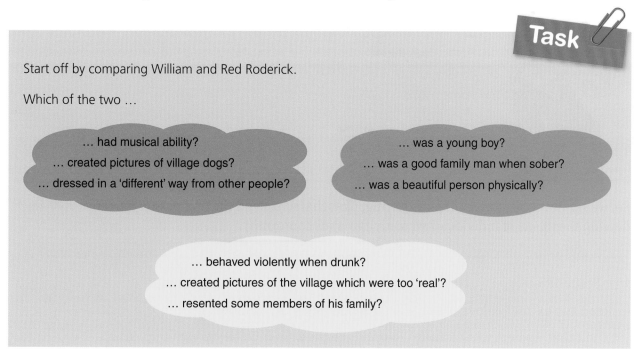

Task

Start off by comparing William and Red Roderick.

Which of the two …

… had musical ability?

… created pictures of village dogs?

… dressed in a 'different' way from other people?

… was a young boy?

… was a good family man when sober?

… was a beautiful person physically?

… behaved violently when drunk?

… created pictures of the village which were too 'real'?

… resented some members of his family?

Task

Now, look at their final significant actions in the story (the **climax** of the story).

Red Roderick: had a violent fight with his father-in-law (involving scythes) in front of the whole village

William Murray: painted a picture of the fight and the villagers watching it excitedly

Why do you think Red Roderick is forgiven and accepted by the village but William Murray is rejected? (Look at the list you have made of his role in the story as well as his final action.)

Possible answer

Red Roderick's behaviour is bad – and the village does not approve – but he does not challenge the community's attitudes or views of itself. In fact, with his music and his hard work (when sober) he contributes positively to village life. He can be criticised but accepted.

William, on the other hand, though he commits no crimes, breaks the village 'rules' by revealing a disturbing truth: that these 'decent, law-abiding' people actually enjoy the vicious fight at the end. By sitting, calmly observing the fight and their 'lust and happiness', he not only separates himself from everyone else but is, in his painting, forcing them to see themselves as they are – fiercely enjoying the violence of the fight. The narrator's actions – attacking William and destroying the painting – illustrate the community's rejection of William's creativity, when used against them. And we hear that he later left the village.

So, we see how Crichton Smith uses setting, plot, characters and the first person narrative style to develop the theme of individuality/creativity versus conformity.

'The Painter'

Read the extract below and answer the questions that follow.

1   But that was not what I meant to tell since the fight in itself, though unpleasant,
    was not evil. No, as I stood in the ring with the others, excited and horrified, I saw on
    the edge of the ring young William with his paint-brush and canvas and easel painting
    the fight. He was sitting comfortably on a chair which he had taken with him and there
5   was no expression on his face at all but a cold clear intensity which bothered me. It
    seemed in a strange way as if we were asleep. As the scythes swung to and fro, as the →

faces of the antagonists became more and more contorted in the fury of battle, as their cheeks were suffused with blood and rage, and their teeth were drawn back in a snarl, he sat there painting the battle, nor at any time did he make any attempt to pull his chair back
10 from the arena where they were engaged.

I cannot explain to you the feelings that seethed through me as I watched him. One feeling was partly admiration that he should be able to concentrate with such intensity that he didn't seem able to notice the danger he was in. The other feeling was one of the most bitter disgust as if I were watching a gaze that had gone beyond the human and which was
15 as indifferent to the outcome as a hawk's might be. You may think I was wrong in what I did next. I deliberately came up behind him and upset the chair so that he fell down head over heels in the middle of a brush-stroke. He turned on me with such a gaze of blind fury that I was reminded of a rat which had once leaped at me from a river bank, and he would have struck me but that I pinioned his arms behind his back. I would have beaten him if
20 his mother hadn't come and taken him away, still snarling and weeping tears of rage. In spite of my almost religious fear at that moment, I tore the painting into small pieces and scattered them about the earth. Some people have since said that what I wanted to do was to protect the good name of the village but I must in all honesty say that that was not in my mind when I pushed the chair over. All that was in my mind was fury and disgust that
25 this painter should have watched this fight with such cold concentration that he seemed to think that the fight had been set up for him to paint, much as a house exists or an old wall.

It is true that after this no one would speak to our wonderful painter; we felt in him a presence more disturbing than that of Red Roderick who did after all recover. So disturbed were we by the incident that we would not even retain the happy paintings he had once
30 painted and which we had bought from him, those of the snow and the harvest, but tore them up and threw them on the dung heap. When he grew up the boy left the village and never returned. I do not know whether or not he has continued as a painter. I must say however that I have never regretted what I did that day and indeed I admire myself for having had the courage to do it when I remember that light, brooding with thunder, and see
35 again in my mind's eye the varying expressions of lust and happiness on the faces of our villagers, many of whom are in their better moments decent and law-abiding men.

Questions

National 5 exam-style questions

1. Look again at lines 1–10.
   In your own words, describe the contrast between the behaviour of William and the other villagers during the fight. **(2 marks)**
2. Look again at lines 11–15 ('… might be.').
   Show how language is used to convey the narrator's feelings at this point in the story. **(2 marks)**
3. 'You may think I was wrong in what I did next.' (lines 15–16)
   In your own words explain what the narrator did. **(2 marks)**
4. Look again at lines 16–22 ('I deliberately came up … the earth.').
   Show how word choice is used to convey the intensity of feelings experienced by both the painter and the narrator. **(4 marks)**
5. 'I have never regretted what I did.' (line 33).
   In your own words, explain why the narrator does not regret his action. **(2 marks)**

Final question

6. Crichton Smith's stories often end with a dramatic climax. By referring to this and at least one other story you have read, show how he achieves this. **(8 marks)**

Possible answers

1. Other villagers: thrilled though appalled by violence **(1 mark)**

   William: clinically/coolly observing **(1 mark)**

2. Examples include:

   'seethed' **(1 mark)** suggests rush of emotion/anger flowing through him **(1 mark)**

   'admiration' **(1 mark)** acknowledges painter's extraordinary, 'cool' quality **(1 mark)**

   'bitter' **(1 mark)** suggests intensity of negative feelings **(1 mark)**

   'disgust' **(1 mark)** revolted by William's calm observation **(1 mark)**

3. Violence towards or restraint of William **(1 mark)**

   Destruction of painting **(1 mark)**

4. Possible answers:

   Painter:
   - 'snarling' **(1 mark)** suggests animal-like fury **(1 mark)**
   - 'tears of rage' **(1 mark)** suggests overwhelmed by anger **(1 mark)**

   Narrator:
   - 'most bitter disgust' **(1 mark)** suggests intensity of revolted feelings **(1 mark)**

5. Remembers villagers' enjoyment of violence **(1 mark)**

   Painting would have depicted this/they were normally 'good' people/would not want to face truth about themselves **(1 mark)**

6. Commonality – **up to 2 marks**: climax allows development of theme/situation between characters to reach moment of maximum impact on reader

   Up to 2 marks for 'The Painter': drama of painter rejected by community shows difficulty of creative person living in world where people have to conform

   Up to 4 marks for other stories, e.g. 'Mother and Son': dramatic climax as John advances towards the bed to take revenge + reference/quote

   'The Telegram': build-up of emotions as mothers watch the elder approaching with the telegram + reference/quote

   'The Crater': build up of tension as Mackinnon and soldiers search for and try to rescue Morrison + reference/quote.

Questions

Higher exam-style questions

1. Look at lines 1–10.
   a) Explain the contrast between William and the rest of the community or the combatants, during the fight. **(2 marks)**
   b) Analyse how language is used to convey this contrast. **(4 marks)**

Final question

2. Crichton Smith's stories often end with a dramatic climax. By referring to this and at least one other story you have read, show how he achieves this. **(10 marks)**

(This question would be suitable for both National 5 and Higher. The standard of answer will be different at Higher.)

Possible answers

1. a) William: detached/focused on capturing spectacle of violence/unemotional **(1 mark)**
      Rest of community: thrilled though appalled by violence **(1 mark)**
      OR
      Combatants: caught up in the savagery of the fight **(1 mark)**
   b) For full marks, both sides of contrast must be shown. 2 marks for detailed/insightful
      comment + reference; 1 mark for more basic comment + reference; 0 marks for reference alone.
      Examples include:
      'excited and horrified' – combination of shock and 'guilty pleasure' in watching fight. Idea of
      thrilled 'excited' comes first, suggesting this is dominant emotion
      'cheeks suffused with blood' – their physical reaction to fighting – blood vessels pounding with
      blood as they attack each other
      'more and more contorted' – repetition – builds up sense of their growing rage and violence
      versus
      William: 'sitting comfortably on a chair' – suggests relaxed and at ease – as if at home
      'cold clear intensity' – word choice reinforced by alliteration – absolute focus of the artist, not
      reacting 'normally' like a human being.

Final question

2. **Up to 2 marks** can be achieved for identifying elements of commonality as identified in the
   question, i.e. stories ending with a dramatic climax. A **further 2 marks** can be achieved for
   reference to the extract given. **6 additional marks** can be awarded for discussion of similar
   references to at least one other short story by Crichton Smith.

   In practice this means:

   - Identification of commonality **(up to 2 marks)** – dramatic climax
     E.g. Crichton Smith often builds up the tension to a dramatic climax at the end of the story.
     This could be a crisis for the main character, a revelation or a moment of clarity **(2 marks)**

   From the extract:

   - **Up to 2 marks** for comment on dramatic climactic ending of 'The Painter'
     E.g. The narrator's disgust and horror at the sight of the painter painting the fight reaches a
     climax when he destroys the painting and attacks William. This reflects the climax in the conflict
     between the painter's creative individuality and the social expectations of the village **(2 marks)**

   From at least one other text:

   - As above (x3) for **up to 6 marks**
   OR
   - More detailed comment (x2) for **up to 6 marks**

   Thus, the final 6 marks can be gained by a combination of 3, 2 and 1 marks, depending on the
   level of depth/detail/insight. The aim would be to encourage quality of comment, rather than
   quantity of references.

   In comments on other texts, possible references include:

   - 'In Church': unease of MacLeod builds up to dramatic shooting by deserter, who has trapped him
     in the pew, listening to the climax of his sermon
   - 'The Telegram': women's fears build up as elder draws closer, ends up passing their houses after
     they have experienced growing agony at the thought of their sons' deaths
   - 'Mother and Son': John's frustration builds until he approaches mother's bed to take revenge,
     then turns instead to look outside, at world he cannot enjoy.

'The Red Door'

This is the final story in the selection, so your study this time will be more independent.

Task

Identify the major theme of this story and discuss/make notes on how plot, setting and characters are used to develop this theme.

Hint!

You can start by listing the main events of the plot and identifying the climax – this will start you off in exploring how the theme is developed through plot.

Task

Next, make a list of characters (obviously there is one definite main character here) and explain why each is important.

The red door itself is a symbol, representing an important idea in the story. Explain how this works.

Possible answers

The plot is very simple: Murdo finds that his door has been painted red and examines his attitudes to life as a result. Set in the small, island community, the story explores the theme of individuality versus conformity. Murdo's decisions – not to re-paint the door and, instead, to knock on Mary's door – show that he is 'becoming himself', an individual. The red door is a symbol of daring new beginnings.

Focus on character: we will have a closer look at the language used to describe Murdo. (Remember that analysis of language will form an important part of your Scottish text question in the exam.)

Notice that Murdo (unlike William Murray in 'The Painter') is not a 'special', creative person. But he, too, struggles to live a happy, fulfilled life in the small community. Yet it is all he has ever known: leaving the village – or breaking its rules on conformity – will take great courage and determination.

Read the quotations below and match each one with an explanation of what it tells us about Murdo's feelings and/or personality. Focus on the language used.

1. 'stared at it for a long time, scratching his head slowly'
2. 'his frugally prepared breakfast – porridge, scones and tea'
3. 'maintained a long silence unless he had something of importance to say'
4. 'Murdo had never in his life done anything unusual'
5. 'almost unintelligible exclamation which had been repeated as a sign of his foolishness'
6. 'Most of the time … he spent working on the land in a dull concentrated manner'

And now, from later in the story … notice how his character is developing:

7. 'it seemed to express something in himself which had been deeply buried for years'
8. 'he felt … as if his head were spinning and he were going round in circles'
9. '"I have never," he thought with wonder, "been myself."'
10. 'But really, was he happy? That was the question.'

Explanations

a) Does not particularly enjoy his work, just gets on with it
b) Has settled into a routine of conforming
c) Puzzled, not quick to come to conclusions
d) Basic lifestyle – nothing fancy – conventional
e) Quiet and does not push himself forward
f) Ridiculed as a child for doing something spontaneous and unusual
g) Sudden epiphany – he has not lived a full life, true to his own identity
h) Questions his assumptions about what has made him feel good in his life
i) Confused and unsure because of these new feelings
j) Experiences feelings he has not felt for a long time

1	2	3	4	5	6	7	8	9	10

Answers

1	2	3	4	5	6	7	8	9	10
c	d	e	b	f	a	j	i	g	h

Murdo's choice to call on Mary at the end marks the start of a new chapter in his life. Why is she so important? Try to find five things about Mary which make her different from other people in the village. And then discuss: why is Murdo attracted to her? What does this suggest about him?

Possible answers

Mary: artistic, reads books, goes for night-time walks alone, does not gossip, enjoys poetry, does not bother about her appearance, independent, gets angry

The fact that Murdo is attracted to her says something about him too: perhaps she has the courage to 'be herself' – courage he has (so far) lacked. She is different; she does not care what others think.

'The Red Door'

Read the extract below and answer the questions that follow.

1   Murdo stared at the door and as he looked at it he seemed to be drawn inside it into its
deep caves with all sorts of veins and passages. It was like a magic door out of the village
but at the same time it pulsed with a deep red light which made it appear alive. It was very
odd and very puzzling, to think that a red door could make such a difference to house and
5   moors and streams.

Solid and heavy he stood in front of it in his wellingtons, scratching his head. But the red
door was not a mirror and he couldn't see himself in it. Rather he was sucked into it as if it
were a place of heat and colour and reality. But it was different and it was his.

It was true that the villagers when they awoke would see it and perhaps make fun of it, and
10   would advise him to repaint it. They might not even want him in the village if he insisted on
having a red door. Still they could all have red doors if they wanted to. Or they could hunt
him out of the village.

Hunt him out of the village? He paused for a moment, stunned by the thought. It had never
occurred to him that he could leave the village, especially at his age, forty-six. But then
15   other people had left the village and some had prospered though it was true that many had
failed. As for himself, he could work hard, he had always done so. And perhaps he had never
really belonged to the village. Perhaps his belonging had been like the Hallowe'en mask. If
he were a true villager would he like the door so much? Other villagers would have been
angry if their door had been painted red in the night, their anger reflected in the red door,
20   but he didn't feel at all angry, in fact he felt admiration that someone should actually have
thought of this, should actually have seen the possibility of a red door, in a green and black
landscape.

He felt a certain childlikeness stirring within him as if he were on Christmas day stealing
barefooted over the cold red linoleum to the stocking hanging at the chimney, to see if
25   Santa Claus had come in the night while he slept.

Having studied the door for a while and having had a long look round the village which was
rousing itself to a new day, repetitive as all the previous ones, he turned into the house. He
ate his breakfast and thinking carefully and joyously and having washed the dishes he set
off to see Mary though in fact it was still early.

30   His wellingtons creaked among the sparkling frost. Its virginal new diamonds glittered
around him, millions of them. Before he knocked on her door he looked at his own door
from a distance. It shone bravely against the frost and the drab patches without frost or
snow. There was pride and spirit about it. It had emerged out of the old and the habitual,
brightly and vulnerably. It said, 'Please let me live my own life.' He knocked on the door.

Questions

National 5 exam-style questions

1. 'Murdo stared at the door.' Look at lines 1–8.
   Show how language is used to suggest that the door is special. **(2 marks)**
2. Look at lines 9–18 (to 'would he like the door so much?').
   Explain in your own words how the red door leads Murdo to consider leaving the village. **(2 marks)**
3. Look at lines 18–22 (from 'Other villagers … landscape').
   Explain how Murdo's reaction to the door differs from how he thinks other villagers would react. **(2 marks)**
4. Look at lines 23–25.
   Show how the writer uses language to reveal Murdo's feelings of excitement in these lines. **(2 marks)**
5. By referring to the final paragraph ('His wellingtons …') show how language is used to show
   Murdo's new way of viewing the world. **(4 marks)**

Final question

6. In his stories, Crichton Smith often develops the theme of individuality versus conformity.
   By referring to this and at least one other story, show how he does this. **(8 marks)**

Possible answers

1. 'magic door' **(1 mark)** imaginary/fairytale **(1 mark)**

   'pulsed' **(1 mark)** living, promise of new life **(1 mark)**

   'deep caves' **(1 mark)** imagination sparked by endless possibilities it represents **(1 mark)**

2. He expects villagers to react negatively to it/to want it changed/they might want him to leave village **(1 mark)**

   This makes him examine possibility of leaving/realise that he might do well if he leaves **(1 mark)**

3. Others would be annoyed **(1 mark)**

   He approves of it/thinks it has been skilfully done **(1 mark)**

4. 'Childlikeness'/'stirring in him'/'Christmas day'/'stealing barefooted'/'to see if Santa had come' **(1 mark)** suggests reawakened excitement in life – as children would feel at Christmas **(1 mark)**

5. Word choice/imagery: 'sparkling frost'/'virginal'/'diamonds'/'glittered'/'It [the door] said, "Please let me live my own life"' – personification **(any one for 1 mark each)**

   Suggesting feeling of excitement/new beginnings/glowing future/door speaks for him in its aspirations towards individuality **(1 mark)**

6. Commonality: stories suggest it is difficult to be an individual/express yourself **(1 mark)** especially in small community where there is pressure to conform **(1 mark)**

   This story: Murdo has lived his whole life 'by the rules' but not been really happy **(1 mark)**; red door makes him realise he may have to leave the village to be himself **(1 mark)**

   Other stories **(up to 4 marks)**. Possible points include:

   - 'The Painter': rejected by community because he 'broke their rules'
   - 'Mother and Son': John longs for freedom to be himself but is trapped in expectation he will care for his mother.

Questions

Higher exam-style questions

1. Look at lines 1–8.
   a) Explain two effects the red door is having on Murdo at this point. **(2 marks)**
   b) Analyse how language is used to convey the impact of the door on him. **(4 marks)**
2. Look at lines 23–25.
   Explain the effect of the references to Christmas at this point. **(2 marks)**

Final question

3. In his stories, Crichton Smith often develops the theme of individuality versus conformity.
   By referring to this and at least one other story, show how he does this. **(10 marks)**

(This question would be suitable for both National 5 and Higher. The standard of answer will be different at Higher.)

Possible answers

1. **a)** He is caught up in it/captivated by it
   He identifies with it/feels it is part of him
   He sees it as a doorway to another world/to freedom
   Any 2 for 1 mark each (2 marks)

   b) 'deep caves' – sense of mystery/'veins and passages' – its wooden texture is transformed by his imagination into an escape route/'magic door' – out of this world/fairytale/possibility of entering another dimension/'pulsed' – alive with potential/'deep red light' – suggestive of life, passion, excitement
   2 marks for detailed/insightful answer + reference (x2 for 4 marks); 1 mark for more basic answer + reference; 0 marks for reference alone

2. Christmas: echoes of happier times/times of excitement/opportunity to regain that feeling of being young and alive/sense of opportunity and anticipation **(Any 2 for 1 mark each)**

Final question

3. **Up to 2 marks** can be achieved for identifying elements of commonality as identified in the question, i.e. theme of individuality versus conformity. A **further 2 marks** can be achieved for reference to the extract given. **6 additional marks** can be awarded for discussion of similar references to at least one other short story by Crichton Smith.

   In practice this means:

   - Identification of commonality **(up to 2 marks)** – individuality versus conformity
     E.g. How difficult it is for a person to 'go against' the community view in order to 'be' him/herself **(2 marks)**

   From the extract:

   - **Up to 2 marks** for comment on theme of individuality versus conformity
     E.g. Murdo realises that his conformity might always have been like a 'Hallowe'en mask', hiding his true feelings. He might never have been happy following the 'rules' of community behaviour **(2 marks)**

   From at least one other text:

   - As above (x3) for **up to 6 marks**

   OR

   - More detailed comment (x2) for **up to 6 marks**

Thus, the final 6 marks can be gained by a combination of 3, 2 and 1 marks, depending on the level of depth/detail/insight. The aim would be to encourage quality of comment, rather than quantity of references.

In comments on other texts, possible references include:

- 'The Painter': rejected by community because he 'broke their rules'/his need to create was more important to him than the community's sense of itself
- 'Mother and Son': John longs for freedom to be himself but is trapped in expectation he will care for his mother
- 'The Telegram': thin woman sending son to university is frowned on by community who see this as 'getting above herself'.

Making connections

Some final thoughts on the stories of Iain Crichton Smith …

Here are some links between the stories, which will help you in the final Scottish text question.

War: 'The Telegram', 'In Church', 'The Crater'

Life in a small community: 'The Telegram', 'The Painter', 'Mother and Son', 'The Red Door'

Individuality versus conformity: 'The Telegram', 'The Painter', 'Mother and Son', 'The Red Door'

Parent/child relationships: 'Mother and Son', 'The Painter', 'The Telegram', 'The Red Door'

Courage/heroism/standing up for self: 'The Crater', 'The Telegram', 'The Red Door', 'The Painter', 'Mother and Son', 'In Church'

Characters who are similar: Mackinnon, MacLeod, Murdo, John ('Mother and Son')

Characters suffering because of environment: John ('Mother and Son'), Morrison, 'priest', William Murray ('The Painter')

Characters who refuse to conform: William Murray, Mary ('The Red Door'), Murdo (at the end)

Stories in which setting is important: All of them

Stories which have dramatic endings/climax: All of them

Stories in which suspense is built up: All of them

Endings involving tragedy/sadness: All but 'The Red Door'

Endings with an element of hope/acceptance: 'The Red Door', 'Mother and Son', 'The Crater', 'The Painter'

CHAPTER 4
NORMAN MACCAIG

Task

Before reading...

With a partner, you are going to do a little research on the great man who created these wonderful poems.

Try to find out three pieces of information on:

- his life
- his beliefs and interests
- his work (writing and other).

Here are some online resources to use:

- www.scottishpoetrylibrary.org.uk
- www.bbc.co.uk – factual arts, culture and the media
- www.poetryfoundation.org

If you want to see and hear him talking, try:

'Off the page', Norman MacCaig

http://tinyurl.com/kkl4a87

(This is quite a long interview so you might like to watch an extract.)

Text list

There are six poems in this collection. MacCaig's poems here deal with people, places, animals – our attitudes to these and to aspects of the 'human condition' (for example, what it means to be human, and the challenges that face us).

'Assisi': an encounter with a disabled beggar outside the church of St Francis of Assisi makes the speaker question our attitudes to others.

'Basking Shark': the encounter this time is with a very primitive animal, a basking shark – again, uncomfortable truths about humanity and nature emerge.

'Visiting Hour': description of a visit to a loved one in hospital explores the fear, sense of loss and pain experienced by the visitor.

'Aunt Julia': memories of a remarkable woman prompt regret about how difficult it can be to communicate with each other.

'Sounds of the Day': the end of a relationship, with a sense of loss and finality.

'Memorial': this time the finality is caused by the death of a loved one; grief of the person left behind is explored.

Thematic links

There are various thematic and stylistic links between these poems. Here are two thematic links to start you off:

The 'human condition'	Love and loss
• 'Assisi'	• 'Visiting Hour'
• 'Basking Shark'	• 'Aunt Julia'
	• 'Sounds of the Day'
	• 'Memorial'

You might want to read all six poems through first, to form your initial impressions of them. This chapter will take you through a detailed study of each individual poem – and remember you should be thinking about connections between them (for that final 8-mark question in the National 5 exam or 10-mark question if you are doing Higher).

'Assisi'

This is one of MacCaig's most famous poems – and it's easy to see why it is so popular. Based on a real-life event when MacCaig visited the Italian town of Assisi, the poem starts from an 'everyday' experience which we could all share (seeing a beggar, ignored by people around him). MacCaig uses this brilliant piece of poetry to examine our attitudes to others. It makes uncomfortable reading, especially at the end, when he turns the spotlight on the reader's own – perhaps complacent – reactions. It is easy to criticise the hypocrisy of others – but disturbing to have to ask if we would do anything better!

Google search 'St Francis of Assisi'. It's quite important to understand what he believed in and stood for, in order to grasp what MacCaig is up to in this poem.

Textual explosion!

This way of adding notes to a text will help you to see the techniques in action.

Read the opening section of the poem and the comment boxes below.

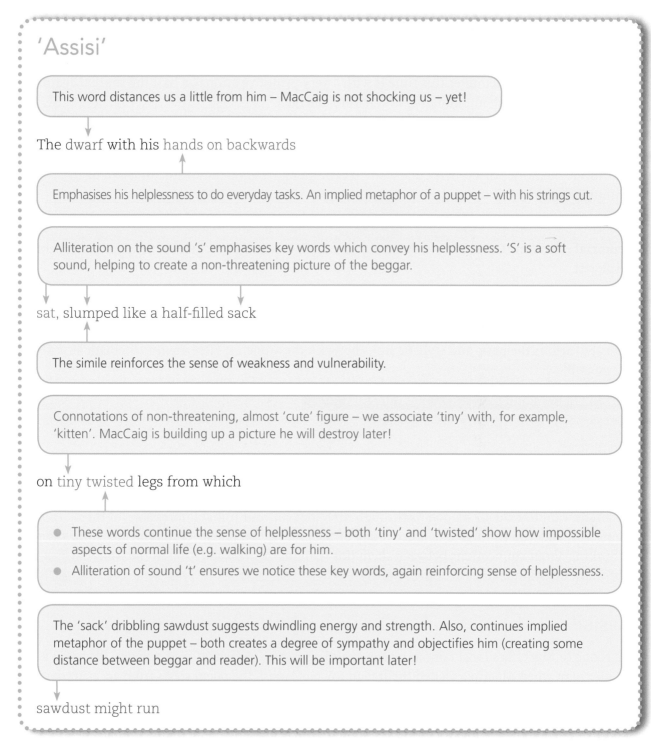

'Assisi'

This word distances us a little from him – MacCaig is not shocking us – yet!

The dwarf with his hands on backwards

Emphasises his helplessness to do everyday tasks. An implied metaphor of a puppet – with his strings cut.

Alliteration on the sound 's' emphasises key words which convey his helplessness. 'S' is a soft sound, helping to create a non-threatening picture of the beggar.

sat, slumped like a half-filled sack

The simile reinforces the sense of weakness and vulnerability.

Connotations of non-threatening, almost 'cute' figure – we associate 'tiny' with, for example, 'kitten'. MacCaig is building up a picture he will destroy later!

on tiny twisted legs from which

- These words continue the sense of helplessness – both 'tiny' and 'twisted' show how impossible aspects of normal life (e.g. walking) are for him.
- Alliteration of sound 't' ensures we notice these key words, again reinforcing sense of helplessness.

The 'sack' dribbling sawdust suggests dwindling energy and strength. Also, continues implied metaphor of the puppet – both creates a degree of sympathy and objectifies him (creating some distance between beggar and reader). This will be important later!

sawdust might run

That's a lot from four lines!

TQE exercise

Have a go at identifying techniques in the rest of stanza 1 (lines 5–9). In pairs, fill in the blanks using Technique (T), Quotation (Q), Effect (E). Some have been done for you.

Technique (T)	Quotation (Q)	Effect (E)
Line 5 Word choice	'outside'	Double meaning: literal = sitting outside church building; metaphorical = outside the 'care' of the church/human society
Line 5 Position of word	'outside'	Acts as a 'pivot' between description of the beggar and the church, emphasising the contrast between them
Line 5 Metaphor	'Three tiers of churches'	
Lines 6–7	'brother of the poor, talker with birds'	Slogan effect, suggesting insincerity
Lines 7–8 Enjambment		Building up to climax/anti-climax at the end
Line 9 Word choice: anti-climax	'Not … dead yet'	

Theme/analysis summary

From your reading of stanza 1 (and your research on St Francis), identify a theme which you feel MacCaig is exploring in this poem. One aspect you may wish to focus on is contrast: the contrast between the pitiful, insignificant beggar and the magnificent church in honour of St Francis. Which techniques are used to establish this contrast? What point is MacCaig making through his use of contrast?

If you can answer these questions, you are well on your way to successful understanding of theme and analysis of techniques. Very important for your critical reading exam!

Let's move on to stanza 2, in which MacCaig leads us into the church, which is full of splendid and valuable artwork.

Research

Google search 'Giotto'. What does this add to your understanding of the poem?

It is important to understand that, hundreds of years ago, most people could not read and relied on artwork such as Giotto's frescoes to make sense of Bible stories. Nowadays, most of us are lucky enough to be educated and should be able to understand the world around us.

Textual explosion!

The second stanza of the poem has been expanded for you.

> **Word choice:** active verb, putting the priest in charge of situation

A priest explained

> **Word choice:** connotations of trickery, manipulation. Also, quite a childish word

How clever it was of Giotto

> **Word choice:** continues the idea of childishness and trickery ('tell stories' is a child's way of saying 'tell lies')

To make his frescoes tell stories

That would reveal to the illiterate the goodness

> **Word position:** why is this word sticking out?

> Combined alliteration and jaunty rhythm (many light stresses) reminds us of the language of advertising

of God and the suffering

of His Son. I understood

> **Sound effect:** echoes the 'good' in 'goodness'
>
> **Word choice:** 'understood' suggests 'saw through'

> **Enjambment:** helps to build up to climax of final line

the explanation and the cleverness

> **Sound effect:** echoes the 'ness' in 'goodness'

Theme/analysis

Again, there is a lot going on in this short verse. With a partner, work out how the theme in stanza 1 is developed further in stanza 2. Think of the priest as a modern-day representative of St Francis' ideals. Look at the techniques highlighted above to help you work out how MacCaig uses language to develop this theme further.

Now to the final stanza.

Stanza 3 begins with an extended metaphor, comparing the tourists to chickens.

> A rush of tourists, clucking contentedly,
>
> Fluttered after him as he scattered
>
> The grain of the Word.

Research

Google the parable of the Sower.

For discussion

What is MacCaig suggesting about the tourists by comparing them to chickens?

What are they 'gobbling up' as they follow the priest?

From your research on the parable of the Sower, what point is MacCaig making by his reference to 'The grain of the Word'?

Possible answer

Chickens are associated with empty-headedness and these tourists are, metaphorically, 'swallowing' whatever the priest tells them. The parable of the Sower is a story told by Jesus in the Bible, to illustrate the power of God's word to take root and flourish in people's minds – so there is an irony in saying that the tourists are swallowing this – when in reality, they are just being taken in by the 'sales pitch' of the priest.

Having suggested how thoughtlessly self-centred the tourists are, MacCaig reinforces this idea in the next two lines:

... It was they who had passed

the ruined temple outside ...

Questions

1. What effect does MacCaig gain by emphasising 'they' in 'it was they who had passed'?
2. The 'ruined temple' is the beggar.
   Why is he compared to a temple? (What would have been the difference if MacCaig had compared him to some other form of building, e.g. a shed?)
   Why is he described as 'ruined'? (This is probably a bit easier.)
3. Why does the word 'outside' appear again? (Remember stanza 1.)

Possible answers

MacCaig focuses on the responsibility of the tourists with 'It was they ...'. The beggar is given a certain dignity by comparing him to a 'temple' (a building with spiritual significance) – albeit a 'ruined' one. And his status as outcast is reinforced by 'outside'.

Now for the big finish!

It was mentioned earlier that the ending of this poem is very important: here's why.

Read from 'It was they ...' again (line 3 of stanza 3) to the end of the poem. Try to focus on how you **feel** as you read it, especially 'whose eyes wept pus, whose back was higher than his head, whose lopsided mouth ...' How is this description different from the one in stanza 1?

The obvious answer is that, in stanza 3, MacCaig deliberately shocks us with the details of how horrific the beggar looks. As we read 'eyes wept pus', how do we feel? Sorry for him, of course, but isn't there also a tiny reaction of disgust too? And this is where the brilliance of the poem lies: we may have been, in our minds, criticising the tourists, the priest, everyone else for ignoring this poor beggar, and then we are forced to ask ourselves, would we have done any differently? The answer, horribly, is probably no. He is not some cute little kitten or baby ... he is hideous and we would probably judge him by his appearance, just as the tourists did – and avoid him. And then, just when we're realising this unpleasant truth, MacCaig hits us with something which makes us feel even more guilty: the man's personality.

> ... whose lopsided mouth
>
> said 'Grazie' in a voice as sweet
>
> as a child's when she speaks to her mother
>
> or a bird's when it spoke
>
> to St Francis

Questions

1. What impression of the beggar's personality are we given?
2. How do the following help create this impression of his personality:
   a) the word 'Grazie'
   b) the comparison with a child and her mother
   c) the comparison with a bird and St Francis?
3. Why do you think MacCaig ended the poem with a final reference to St Francis?

Possible answers

He is a sweet, grateful, appreciative and innocent person, as shown by 2 a), b) and c). Bringing the poem round to St Francis at the end reminds us of that good man's spiritual and caring ideals – reinforcing the idea that the world is a hard, uncaring and spiritually empty place.

TQE exercise

Here's a final TQE exercise, to consolidate what you've learned about stanza 3.
Note: these line numbers refer to lines **within** stanza 3.

Technique	Quotation	Effect
Lines 1–3 Extended metaphor		Suggests tourists are empty-headed, unable to sympathise with others
Lines 2–3 Allusion (biblical)	'scattered/The grain of the Word'	
Line 3 Sentence structure		Puts emphasis on 'them', the tourists, reinforcing their responsibility
Line 4	'ruined temple'	Beggar is terrible condition, like a ruin, but he still has spiritual value, like a temple
Lines 4–5 Word choice		Shocks the reader
Lines 4–6 Repetitive sentence structure	'Whose eyes … whose back … whose lopsided'	
Line 7 Word choice		Suggests the beggar is a grateful man who appreciates life despite his suffering
Lines 7–8 Simile	'a voice as sweet/as a child's when she speaks to her mother'	
Lines 8–9 Simile		Suggests that the beggar is as innocent as a bird/suggests connection with St Francis' caring message
Last line Stanza structure: climax	'to St Francis'	

A few final thoughts …

This is a poem that uses contrast effectively throughout. One contrast we are left thinking about is between the beautiful church/artwork and the beggar: which of them more truly reflects the message of St Francis – or, indeed, any message about treating other people decently and kindly? The beggar has a terrible life – probably in constant pain, being rejected, treated with no dignity whatsoever, yet MacCaig suggests that, despite it all, he is sweet, kind, appreciative. So he – by his very attitude and personality – teaches more about faith, love and goodness than any amount of beautiful art. Whether you view the ending as positive (how amazing that he can retain such good qualities!) or negative (how can we be so unfair and superficial in our judgements of others?) is up to you.

Now, a chance to practise your analysis skills in an exam-style question. If you have read only 'Assisi', you should be able to answer questions 1–4. If you have read others in the selection, you could also have a go at question 5, which asks you to go beyond 'Assisi' to other poems. Discuss with your partner which poems might be suitable for linking with 'Assisi'. In this example, the linking area (or 'commonality' as SQA calls it) is: poems which start from an 'ordinary' experience and move on to make a comment about him.

Questions

National 5 exam-style questions

1. Show how MacCaig uses poetic techniques to convey the contrast between the beggar and the church in stanza 1. **(4 marks)**
2. Explain MacCaig's use of the word 'outside' in stanza 1. **(2 marks)**
3. Show how imagery is used to convey MacCaig's attitude to the tourists in stanza 3. **(2 marks)**
4. By referring to the final lines of the poem (from 'whose eyes …') show how language is used to create an effective ending. **(4 marks)**

Final question

5. MacCaig's poetry often begins from an experience anyone might have and then moves on to develop an idea. By referring to this and at least one other poem, show how he uses 'ordinary' experience to develop ideas. **(8 marks)**

Possible answers

1. Beggar: simile 'slumped like a half-filled sack'/word choice 'hands on backwards' or 'tiny, twisted' alliteration 'tiny, twisted'/word choice/order 'not being dead yet' **(1 mark)** suggests weak, pitiful, insignificant, neglected, etc. person **(1 mark)**

   Church: wedding cake metaphor 'three tiers of churches' **(1 mark)** suggests splendid, ornate, imposing, etc. **(1 mark)**

2. Literal: he is physically outside the building **(1 mark)**

   Metaphorical: he is outwith the care of the church/society **(1 mark)**

3. Metaphor of the chickens: various quotations **(1 mark)** suggest he thinks they are thoughtless, empty-headed, don't care for fellow humans **(1 mark)**

   Less likely but still valid: beggar compared to 'ruined temple' **(1 mark)** suggests his dignity as a person which they are ignoring – therefore they are thoughtless **(1 mark)**

4. Word choice to indicate external appearance of beggar, e.g. 'eyes wept pus' **(1 mark)** brutally reinforces the horror of beggar's appearance/forces us to examine our own reactions to him **(1 mark)**

   Contrast with language suggesting internal personality, e.g. 'Grazie'/'voice as sweet as a child's … mother'/ending poem by reference to St Francis **(1 mark)** surprises us with his kind, appreciative personality/brings idea of poem round to true spirit of a man like St Francis **(1 mark)**

5. **Up to 2 marks** for commonality, i.e. use of 'everyday' experience allows him to relate to readers/make a point of universal relevance

   Up to 2 marks for reference to 'Assisi', i.e. experience of seeing beggar/someone less fortunate than ourselves makes us examine our reactions to others/think about how we judge others/exposes hypocrisy

   Up to 4 marks for references to other poems, e.g. 'Visiting Hour': visiting sick person in hospital leads to examination of our fear of loss, thoughts about illness of loved ones and death

   'Basking Shark': surprise encounter leads to rethinking of our relationship with nature, primitive versus civilised in humanity

   'Aunt Julia': memory of childhood visits leads to thoughts on lack of communication, lost opportunities.

Questions

Higher exam-style questions

1. By referring to examples of poetic technique in stanza 1, show how an effective contrast
   is established. **(4 marks)**
2. By referring to ideas and/or language, evaluate how effective you find the final lines
   (from line 4 of stanza 3) as a conclusion to the poem. **(4 marks)**

Final question

3. MacCaig's poetry often universalises individual experience in order to convey a message.
   By referring to this and one or more other poems by MacCaig, show how he does this. **(10 marks)**

Possible answers

1. For full marks both sides of the contrast must be covered. Contrast between pitiful, vulnerable
   beggar (conveyed through, e.g. simile 'sat, slumped like a half-filled sack'; extended, implied
   metaphor of the abandoned puppet; alliteration/word choice of 'tiny, twisted legs' to emphasise
   weakness) and ornate, splendid church ('three tiers of churches' – metaphor of wedding cake
   suggests visually impressive but, ultimately, unnecessary).

   A detailed/insightful comment on one point (+ reference) will be awarded 2 marks; 1 mark for
   more basic comment (plus reference). 4 marks can be awarded 2+2, 2+1+1 or 1+1+1+1. 0 marks
   for quote/reference alone.

2. Ideas: rounds off the poem effectively by forcing the reader to examine own complacency and
   attitudes to those less fortunate.

   Ideas: climax of contrast between beggar's hideous appearance and beautiful personality – develops
   contrast earlier between beautiful cathedral and deformed beggar.

   Language: build up of brutal vocabulary 'eyes wept pus' etc. conveys the horror of man's appearance,
   explains reaction of tourists etc./exposes reaction of reader.

   Language: build up of images linked to purity and love 'like a child's … St Francis' emphasises
   sweetness of beggar's personality, truer reflection of message of St Francis than the artwork.

   A detailed/insightful comment on one point (plus reference) will be awarded 2 marks; 1 mark for
   more basic comment (plus reference). 4 marks can be awarded 2+2, 2+1+1 or 1+1+1+1. 0 marks
   for quote/reference alone.

Final question

3. **Up to 2 marks** can be achieved for identifying elements of commonality as identified in the
   question, i.e. MacCaig's use of individual experience to develop 'universal' theme.

   A **further 2 marks** can be achieved for reference to the extract given.

   6 additional marks can be awarded for discussion of similar references to at least one other poem
   by MacCaig.

   In practice this means:

   - Identification of commonality **(up to 2 marks)** – 'universal' theme
     E.g. Use of individual experience to develop 'universal' theme engages the reader through
     specific, thought-provoking moments which have relevance for us all **(2 marks)**

   From 'Assisi':

   - **Up to 2 marks** for comment on use of individual experience to develop 'universal' theme
     E.g. Experience of seeing the beggar, neglected and disabled, leads to examination of the
     way human beings judge, value and consider others **(2 marks)**

From at least one other poem:

- as above (x3) for **up to 6 marks**

OR

- more detailed comment (x2) for **up to 6 marks**

Thus, the final 6 marks can be gained by a combination of 3, 2 and 1 marks, depending on the level of depth/detail/insight.

Possible references from other poems include:

- 'Basking Shark': encounter with primitive animal makes speaker examine relationship between civilised humans and apparently savage nature
- 'Visiting Hour': painful visit to loved one in hospital conveys our universal helplessness in face of illness and death
- 'Memorial': experience of bereavement, reflection on the devastating nature of human loss, universal and all-consuming

'Basking Shark'

This thought-provoking poem, like 'Assisi', takes as its starting point a real event: an encounter between MacCaig and a basking shark. The sight of this primitive animal prompts him to examine our view of ourselves as human beings, our relationship with nature and our attitudes to evolution. The basking shark is at (or near) one end of the evolutionary spectrum; we see ourselves as existing at the other.

Google search 'basking shark' to find out more about this fascinating animal. It is important to understand that a basking shark is not dangerous – unless it bangs into you, of course! Put thoughts of great white sharks terrorising beaches out of your mind.

Textual explosion!

This way of adding notes to a text helps you to figure out how it works.

Read the opening section of the poem and the comment boxes below.

'Basking Shark'

> Beginning the line with infinitive verb puts emphasis on the word 'stub', showing drama of the moment.

To stub an oar on a rock where none should be,

> Air of mystery created by the syntax and word choice – nothing is revealed yet.

> Repetition of infinitive verb structure, builds up momentum and pace towards final line.

To have it rise with a slounge out of the sea

> 'Slounge': this amazing Scots word combines connotations of 'slow', 'lunge', 'lounge' and 'plunge' suggesting the sound and movement of the huge shark, rising clumsily out of the sea and plunging back in: word choice and onomatopoeia.

> Alliteration of the 's' sound draws attention to this important moment.

> Deliberately clumsy sentence structure creates sense of awkwardness, an uncomfortable memory, also keeps the focus on the moment described in lines 1 and 2.

Is a thing that happened once (too often) to me

> Parenthesis adds a degree of humour to the tone – and a sense that this was a genuinely frightening experience.

Task

Have a go at exploding the next three lines (stanza 2) yourself (or with a partner). Try to get something from every line. Copying it out and using highlighters can be substituted for computer technology if need be!

But not too often – though enough. I count as gain

That once I met, on a sea tin-tacked with rain,

That roomsized monster with a matchbox brain.

What have you found?

Here are some ideas:

1. You probably noticed the disjointed sentence structure and meaning in line 1. 'But not too often – though enough'. Looking back to stanza 1 line 3, it almost looks as if MacCaig is changing his mind on how he felt about the experience as he goes along. Of course he isn't (each word in a poem is carefully chosen) but something is going on. After the supremely controlled infinitive verb structure 'To stub … To have it rise', the syntax seems to break down, suggesting confusion. As we'll see, that's exactly what happens in terms of the speaker's view of himself and humanity: certainty becomes doubt and confusion. So, the sentence structure in these lines is helping to develop a major theme of the poem.

2. '… on a sea tin-tacked with rain'. This phrase combines metaphor with alliteration and onomatopoeia to capture beautifully the moment when the shark appeared. Through the metaphor 'tin-tacked with rain', MacCaig creates the picture of the sharp rain drops hitting relentlessly off the surface of the sea. The alliteration of the sound 't', along with the onomatopoeia of 'tin-tacked', conveys the pinging noise of the raindrops, so emphasising the metaphor itself.

3. '… roomsized monster with a matchbox brain' Effective use of contrast highlights the two most significant aspects of the shark: its huge size (making the encounter a terrifying experience, even though it is not fierce) and its tiny brain: it is a primitive animal, undeveloped since ancient times.

Your own notes may not be as detailed, but just getting into the habit of focusing on the techniques in each line – and how they link to theme – is really important.

Task

TQE exercise

Now, with a partner, try the TQE method on stanzas 3 and 4.

Technique (T)	Quotation (Q)	Effect (E)
Stanza 3, line 1 Word choice: use of Scots onomatopoeia	'shoggled'	Highlights two meanings: literal (nudged the boat) and metaphorical (jogging him out of his complacency). Physical sense of the abrupt thump
Stanza 3, line 2 Word choice	'Decadent townie'	
Stanza 3, line 3 Metaphors (two combined)		Conventional metaphor suggesting family links stretching back becomes a fresh idea: a shaking perch hints that speaker no longer feels secure and safe in his assumptions about his identity
Stanza 4, lines 1–2 Extended metaphor		Emphasises vital point that unsettling our assumptions can lead to greater clarity
Stanza 4, line 2 Paradox	'I saw me'	
Stanza 4, line 2 Word choice	'fling'	
Stanza 4, line 3 Word choice		Echoes movement of shark, coming out of water: suggests revelation of who he really is
Stanza 4, line 3 Metaphor/word choice	'The slime of everything'	

What is happening in this middle section of the poem?

MacCaig moves from describing the actual, physical experience of 'meeting' the shark to considering the psychological impact of the encounter. He compares the displacement of the sea as the shark hauls its huge body to the surface and then down again to the metaphorical displacement of his ideas. The appropriately watery extended metaphor of 'Swish up the dirt and, when it settles, a spring is all the clearer' captures this idea. Just as, if you swirl up water (for example, in a stream or the sea) at first it goes all muddy or sandy – but then settles more clearly, as all the sediment sinks to the bottom – so with our thoughts. MacCaig argues that if our complacent ideas are shaken, we might feel muddled at first, but will see all the more clearly afterwards. Suddenly, MacCaig has an epiphany: he understands something about humanity which he didn't grasp before. But what is it? '… I saw me, in one fling, emerging …' in other words, he sees himself – representing human beings in general, as a part of evolution. We and the basking shark – and every other life form on the planet – have common ancestors. More of this later …

Now for the big finish!

As with 'Assisi', we can expect a 'big finish' in this poem. Let's pause for a second to consider two elements: rhyme and structure.

Rhyme

Unlike 'Assisi', 'Basking Shark' does rhyme – and in an unusual way. Each stanza is made up of three lines (a triplet) all of which rhyme. This is called a tercet. So, the rhyme scheme is AAABBBCCC and so on. What effects does MacCaig achieve by using this rhyming scheme?

Structure

There are five tercets, each one ending on a full stop. This is called end-stopped line (and is the opposite of enjambment). How does this structure combine with rhyme to develop the theme?

We can see that both the structure and use of rhyme create a series of mini-statements. Each stanza is 'bound together' by its rhyme and each one represents a distinct stage in MacCaig's exploration of the experience:

Stanza 1: the first dramatic moment

Stanza 2: atmospheric description of the encounter

Stanza 3: immediate impact on the speaker

Stanza 4: philosophical consequences of the encounter

This is building up effectively to the final stanza, the 'big finish', which leaves us with some disturbing thoughts.

Exploration of stanza 5

In pairs …

1. What is the effect of beginning the stanza with the rhetorical question, 'So who's the monster?'
2. What is the thought that makes the speaker 'go pale' and why does he do so?
3. Why is the time of 'twenty seconds' mentioned?
4. What does the metaphor 'sail after sail' contribute?
5. How does MacCaig 'slow down' the action in the final line of the poem and why does he do so?
6. What are we left thinking at the end of 'Basking Shark'?

This poem, like 'Assisi', prompts us to question our assumptions about ourselves and to examine 'the human condition' – what it means to be a human being. The confrontation between the sophisticated, intelligent speaker (the 'decadent townie') and the huge but tiny-brained shark shakes the comfortable assumptions the speaker normally has. What would these be? That we humans are at the top of the evolutionary 'ladder' and therefore, not only more complex and developed than 'simpler' animals, but also somehow more valuable? That we are in charge of the world and doing a good job?

Seeing the shark emerge from the sea makes the speaker realise that we, too, developed from 'the slime of everything' – the sort of primeval swamp we might associate with the earliest times of life on this planet. We are related to the shark (and other primitive animals) – so, are we all that different? And when we think about it – who has messed up the world: animals like the shark or we 'special' human beings? The answer is obvious – and not very comfortable for us. The shark may look like a 'monster' – but it is a gentle beast, swimming slowly along with its mouth open, swallowing plankton. But, even if it were fierce and aggressive, could it compare with the damage done by humans, both to the planet and to each other? That simple question, 'So who's the monster?' is chillingly effective … No wonder MacCaig went pale!

Task

Get together with another pair to form a larger group and have a go at creating a series of exam-style questions on 'Basking Shark'. (Look back at the questions on 'Assisi' to help you if necessary.) Try for around four questions on 'Basking Shark', focusing on ideas and techniques, and then make up one 8-mark question (or 10-mark question if you are doing Higher) that links this poem to at least one other you have read. If you have read only 'Assisi', that's fine: there are plenty of links that can be made between these two poems.

Try making up 'Marking instructions' and swapping with another group, so they can try your questions and you can try theirs. Then, mark them using your 'Marking instructions'.

Hint!

Speaker/reader forced to examine their assumptions; use of contrast; use of metaphors; unexpected encounter; effective endings …)

'Visiting Hour'

This is one of MacCaig's most widely known and best-loved poems. It's easy to see how anyone can relate to the subject – the pain of visiting a seriously ill loved one in hospital. The poem is, again, based on MacCaig's own personal experience, but he universalises this by the skill of his writing. By focusing on the experience of the senses, the thoughts and feelings of the narrator/visitor and by his acute observation of the hospital itself and the people in it – he creates a wonderful piece that vividly evokes the experience.

The poem is in the form of a journey, along the hospital corridor, towards the ward, then up to the patient in her bed. It ends with the visitor leaving, to begin the return journey. It is also an emotional journey, as the visitor experiences discomfort, anxiety, admiration (of the nurses), fear of loss, pain and, ultimately, despair.

Let's begin by examining the early stages of the journey.

Textual explosion!

This way of adding notes to a text will help you to see the techniques in action.

Read stanza 1 of the poem and the comment boxes below.

'Visiting Hour'

Word choice/structure: (poem begins with these words) emphasises the strong disinfectant smell – something we all relate to.

Metaphor: conveys the forceful, intrusive way the smell impacts on the visitor's nose.

The hospital smell

combs my nostrils

as they go bobbing along

green and yellow corridors

Word choice: 'they' referring to 'nostrils' creates sense of his heightened awareness of smell/depersonalising feeling emphasising anxiety.

Word choice: colours associated with sickness, infection. Reinforces uncomfortable feeling.

Word choice: emphasises sense of movement and awkward feeling of being out of place.

Have a go at exploding stanza 2 yourself (or with a partner). Key words and phrases have been selected for you.

> What seems a corpse
>
> is trundled into a lift and vanishes
>
> heavenward

You might be asking yourself, what did the visitor see? And what did he think he saw?

It is, in fact, very unlikely that a dead person would be moved around the hospital during visiting time – and notice that he says, 'What seems a corpse'. Is he, perhaps, so preoccupied with illness and dying that everything he sees around him makes him think of death?

The word 'corpse' is deliberately clinical, unemotional: keep that in mind as it will be developed further. The word 'trundled' suggests clumsy movement, as if a trolley is bumping over bumps: perhaps disrespectful – certainly businesslike.

What do you make of the final words: 'vanishes/heavenward', used to describe the trolley going up in the lift? 'Vanishes' has connotations of magical disappearance; while 'heavenward' is another reference to death. The speaker is confused, unsure … and negative thoughts are crowding in.

Stanza 3 is very short but full of meaning. Read it over with your partner and make notes under the following headings:

> **Word choice   Repetition   Enjambment   Structure of stanza (building to climax)**

The power of this stanza is in the determination of the speaker not to feel upset, when we can see he is, in fact, already suffering terribly. It's an effective statement of denial. How does MacCaig achieve this?

- Word choice: the simple, direct vocabulary, e.g. 'I will not feel' focuses attention on his pain.

- Repetiton and enjambment, 'not/feel' and 'until/I have', emphasise this feeling further

- The stanza builds to the climactic line, 'I have to', which reinforces the feeling that his suffering is inevitable.

TQE exercise

Let's try a TQE analysis for stanza 4, where the speaker is observing the nurses, moving professionally around the hospital.

(**Note:** the line numbers refer to the lines within stanza 4.)

Technique (T)	Quotation (Q)	Effect (E)
Line 1 Word choice	'lightly, swiftly'	
Line 2 Re-sequencing of normal word order		The nurses seem to be rushing around everywhere: busy and professional
	'slender waists'	Emphasises his amazement that they have the strength to 'carry' the suffering of patients and their families
Line 2 Word choice	'miraculously'	
Lines 4–5, 5–6, 6–7, 7–8 Enjambment		Conveys build up of emotions towards the climax
Lines 6–7 Word choice	'eyes still clear'	
Lines 5, 6, 8	'So much … so many … so many'	Emphasises the number of tragedies they have witnessed and coped with
Line 8 Word choice: climax	'So many farewells' (final line)	

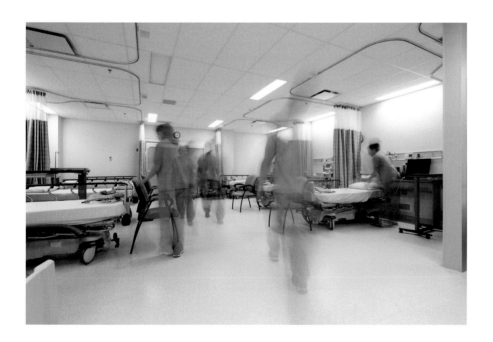

Questions

In stanza 5, he reaches the ward and sees his loved one. We will examine two main aspects of the stanza.

1. **The imagery used to describe the patient.**
   The stanza is dominated by three images: the 'white cave', the 'withered hand' and 'the glass fang'. With your partner, pick one of these. Explain what the image means literally and why it is effective in conveying a sense of this very ill woman.
   Here they are written out in full:

   'She lies/ in a white cave of forgetfulness.'

   'A withered hand/trembles on its stalk'

   'Into an arm wasted

   Of colour a glass fang is fixed,

   Not guzzling but giving'

2. **His realisation that his journey can take him no further, he has come to the end of the journey.**

   'Ward 7.'

   Why do you think MacCaig chose to announce his arrival with this expression?
   How does he emphasise the sheer weakness of the patient?
   Read the final lines of the stanza (from 'And between …') and work out what he is saying about the distance that still exists between them, even when he is standing right next to her hospital bed.

Possible answers

1. **Imagery:**

   - 'white cave of forgetfulness' – refers literally to the white, sterile environment she is in and suggests that her illness or drugged state has cut her off from reality; it is as if she is deep in a cave
   - 'withered hand trembles on its stalk' – refers to a dried up, dying plant and suggests she is now so ill that there seems to be no life in her
   - 'into an arm … giving' – refers to a vampire, which we think of as sucking blood away and suggests that the life-giving drip she is attached to looks predatory

2. **End of the journey:**

   - 'Ward 7' – abruptness – possibly quoting a sign on the wall, suggests he has arrived almost 'too soon' – reluctance to see her suffering
   - The 'distance' is described as a physical barrier between them: in fact, it is a metaphor to show that neither can really share the other's pain (hers is physical; his emotional)

Task

To finish off your analysis of this poem, try to 'explode' the final verse (on the next page).

Hint!

The perspective changes to that of the patient (or, at least, what he thinks her perspective might be). It is almost cinematic: we 'see' him leave, from her point of view and the 'camera' moves round to rest finally on the gifts he has left behind.

She smiles a little at this

black figure in her white cave

who clumsily rises

in the round swimming waves of a bell

and dizzily goes off, growing fainter,

not smaller. Leaving behind only

books that will not be read

and fruitless fruits.

What feeling are we left with at the end of the poem? Try to identify the tone MacCaig creates at the end – and how he does so. (Your 'explosion' ideas will help you here.) Time to try the kind of questions you might face on this poem in your exam. Remember that the final question asks you to 'go beyond' this poem to at least one other poem by MacCaig.

Questions

National 5 exam-style questions

1. In stanza 1, show how MacCaig uses language to create an effective opening to the poem. **(2 marks)**
2. By referring to two techniques, explain how stanza 3 (beginning 'I will not …') shows that he is upset. **(4 marks)**
3. Explain one of the images used in stanza 5 to describe the patient and analyse the effect of the image. **(3 marks)**
4. Identify the tone created in the final stanza and show how language is used to create this tone. **(3 marks)**

Final question

5. MacCaig often uses contrast in his poetry. By referring to this and at least one other poem, show how contrast is used. **(8 marks)**

Possible answers

1. 'hospital smell … combs my nostrils' metaphor **(1 mark)** suggesting invasive, unpleasant smell **(1 mark)**

   OR 'they go bobbing' – use of surprising pronoun 'they' **(1 mark)** suggests depersonalised experience/heightened anxiety **(1 mark)**

   OR 'green and yellow' choice of colours **(1 mark)** suggests sickness **(1 mark)**

2. Repetition of 'I will not' **(1 mark)** suggests determination not to feel (therefore already feeling) **(1 mark)**

   OR enjambment 'not/feel' **(1 mark)** suggests intensity of emotion **(1 mark)**

   OR stating the opposite 'I will not feel' **(1 mark)** suggests cannot face pain **(1 mark)**

   OR short, dramatic final line **(1 mark)** emphasises inevitability of pain coming **(1 mark)**

   Any two techniques plus comments for 4 marks.

3. 'white cave of forgetfulness' – white cave suggests something deep, hidden/refers to white bed linen/sterile environment **(1 mark)**; her illness/drugged state has cut her off from reality; it is as if she is deep in a cave, removed from conscious life and those around her **(up to 2 marks** for full analysis)

   OR 'withered hand trembles on its stalk' – suggests dying plant or cut flower, drying up **(1 mark)**; she is now so weak and ill that there seems to be no life in her, she is just the dried up 'stalk' of a living being **(up to 2 marks** for full analysis)

   OR 'into an arm ... giving' suggests a vampire which we think of as sucking blood/killing **(1 mark)**; although the drip she is attached to is giving her life through blood/fluids, she is so ill that it seems as if the life is being, horrifically, drained out of her **(up to 2 marks** for full analysis)

4. Tone is pessimistic, despairing **(1 mark)**, 'black figure' **(1 mark)** suggests symbol of death (as well as visitor) **(1 mark)**

   OR 'books that will not be read' **(1 mark)** pointlessness of gifts; too weak/possibly dying **(1 mark)**; 'fruitless fruits' – use of pun **(1 mark)** as above

   Please note there may be other correct answers.

5. **Up to 2 marks** for comment on commonality, e.g. contrast is used to highlight differences between characters or to make a comment on aspects of the human condition, perhaps showing us uncomfortable truths

   Up to 2 marks for comments on 'Visiting Hour', e.g. speaker's emotion versus professionalism of nurses; white cave versus black figure

   Up to 4 marks for comments on other poems, e.g. primitive animal versus sophisticated human being in 'Basking Shark'; splendid church versus pitiful beggar in 'Assisi'

Questions

Higher exam-style questions

1. In stanza 1, analyse how MacCaig uses language to introduce a central concern of the poem. **(2 marks)**
2. Choose one of the images used in stanza 4. Analyse your chosen image. **(2 marks)**

Final question

3. MacCaig often uses contrast to develop theme in his poetry. By referring to this and at least one other poem, show how contrast is used to develop theme. **(10 marks)**

(**Note:** there could be a similar question at National 5 level, but the expected response will be different.)

Possible answers

1. Possible answers: 'combs my nostrils' metaphor of 'comb' to describe smell entering his nose suggests invasive, unpleasant smell, creating a sense of his extreme discomfort – introduces idea of the visit as an uncomfortable experience

   'as they go bobbing along' focus on the nostrils' journey along the corridors – rather than his – suggests a feeling of de-personalisation, symptomatic of extreme anxiety or discomfort. It is as if 'he' is not really there, yet at the same time he is experiencing his senses in a heightened way

   A detailed/insightful comment (plus reference) will be awarded 2 marks; 1 mark for more basic comment (plus reference)

2. Possible answer: 'white cave of forgetfulness' – just as cave suggests something 'apart from' or 'separate' and hidden from the normal, outdoor world, so the woman in the hospital bed, surrounded by white sheets and the sterile environment of the hospital appears to be in a white cave. This is a 'cave of forgetfulness' meaning that she is so ill, so weak – or maybe so drugged – that she cannot communicate or concentrate properly

   A detailed/insightful comment (plus reference) will be awarded 2 marks; 1 mark for more basic comment (plus reference)

Final question

3. **Up to 2 marks** for comment on commonality, i.e. contrast is used to highlight differences between characters or to make a comment on aspects of the human condition, perhaps showing us uncomfortable truths

   Up to 2 marks for comments on 'Visiting Hour', e.g. speaker's emotion versus professionalism of nurses OR white cave versus black figure to develop theme of emotional loss

   Up to 6 marks for comments on how contrast is used to develop theme in other poems.

   In practice this means:

   - Identification of commonality **(up to 2 marks)** – use of contrast, e.g. contrast used to highlight differences between characters or to make a comment on aspects of the human condition, perhaps showing us uncomfortable truths

   From 'Visiting Hour':

   - **Up to 2 marks** for comment on use of contrast in 'Visiting Hour', e.g. speaker's emotion is revealed through denial ('I will not feel') – contrasts with the (necessary) professionalism of the nurses. This highlights the extreme emotion he is feeling **(2 marks)**

   From at least one other poem:

   - as above (x3) for **up to 6 marks**

   OR

   - more detailed comment (x2) for **up to 6 marks**

   Thus, the final 6 marks can be gained by a combination of 3, 2 and 1 marks, depending on the level of depth/detail/insight.

   Possible references from other poems include:

   - 'Assisi': splendid church versus pitiful beggar – contrast used to develop idea/theme of hypocrisy

   - 'Aunt Julia': noisy life force that was Aunt Julia versus the silence of her grave – contrast used to develop her character and his sense of regret that she is gone.

'Aunt Julia'

Having developed your analysis skills on the last three poems, it's time to put them into practice independently in your study of poem four, 'Aunt Julia'. This poem is again based on MacCaig's personal experience.

As you'll know from your research, MacCaig lived his whole life in Edinburgh. However, he spent holidays on the remote Hebridean island of Scalpay, where his Aunt Julia lived. She was a Gaelic speaker and MacCaig, as a child, spoke no Gaelic.

This poem deals with three key ideas:

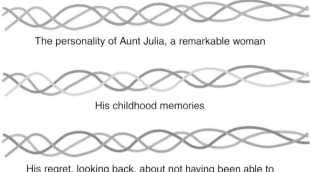

The personality of Aunt Julia, a remarkable woman

His childhood memories

His regret, looking back, about not having been able to communicate with her

In practice, these are not separated out into different parts of the poem, but blended together throughout. MacCaig uses a range of techniques – with which you're now familiar – to develop these ideas effectively. Before you begin: as you're going to work on this poem more independently, here's some help with the 'research' part.

Name	Definition
Spinning wheel	traditional 'machine' for processing rough wool, from the sheep, into thin yarn (balls of wool), for use in knitting. Think 'the sleeping beauty'! No electricity needed: the power is from the spinner's foot, 'paddling the treadle', that is, pressing down onto the metal 'plate' which powers the spinning wheel.
Box bed	in old houses and flats, where accommodation was limited, this would be a bed in a recess in a room used for other purposes (e.g. living room or kitchen). It would be separated from the rest of the room by wooden shutters, pulled across, giving the sleeper privacy: very like a box, in fact.
Brown eggs	more unusual when MacCaig was a child than now (most were white). More likely to find them in the country than in Edinburgh.
Black skirts	traditionally worn by women – they would be long
Threepenny bits	coins from the 'old' days of shillings and half crowns; not very valuable but look distinctive
Luskentyre	located on the island of Harris, a bigger island next to tiny Scalpay
Peatscrapes and lazybeds	traditional crofting methods. Peat: ancient plants, rotted into fibrous matter, cut out of the ground in 'bricks' and left to dry, traditionally, used as fuel. Lazybeds involve growing potatoes without digging; soil and fertiliser (often seaweed) is put on them from nearby.

Part one: DIY analysis

First of all, read the poem. Then undertake the following task.

Task

Form groups of three. Each person will take one of the key ideas above (personality of Aunt Julia, childhood memories, adult regret about lack of communication). If there are more than three people in your group, mini-groups can work on each one.

Using your key idea as a heading, go through the poem looking for examples of techniques used to establish or develop that idea. Note down your examples, using the TQE method, then get together to compare notes. There will be overlap – some examples will develop more than one of the key ideas. Here are some techniques for you to look out for:

- Structure: look out for beginnings and endings (to a line, a stanza, the poem itself). Why did MacCaig choose to use the words he did at these important moments?
- Word choice/descriptive details
- Repetition
- Onomatopoeia
- Alliteration
- Metaphor
- Contrast
- Enjambment

Possible answers

Personality of Aunt Julia

Technique	Effects
Structure	every stanza begins with direct reference to A.J. ('She', 'Hers') – emphasises her importance. First and last stanzas begin 'Aunt Julia' – links these together, brings focus begins and ends firmly with her
Word choice	various examples used to establish/reinforce sense of her as strong, a force of life e.g. 'very loud and very fast'; 'men's boots' (does traditionally 'male' tasks); 'strong foot'; 'stained with peat' (going barefoot outdoors/hardy/at one with nature); 'marvellously'(almost magical quality of her skill); 'keeper of threepennybits/in a teapot' (eccentric, individual, thrifty); 'seagull's voice' (identification with wild nature); 'getting angry' (her powerful emotions, lack of sentimentality); 'peatscrapes and lazybeds' places her firmly in the traditional, natural environment
Repetition	'very loud and very fast': emphasises her emphatic, determined character; 'she was' brings focus to her qualities, his persistent memories of her (and what he associated with her), also emphasises his inability to understand. First and last stanza: repetition of opening two lines shows the importance of her language (and its incomprehensibility)
Onomatopoeia	'paddling the treadle': captures rhythmic movement of the spinning wheel, powered by her foot
Alliteration	'water … winds … wetly': emphasises fluid quality/watery sound of elements he associates with her
Metaphor	various enforcing idea of Aunt Julia as elemental force, at one with air and water and her links with the traditional hard work of the croft: 'She was buckets … them', 'She was … house-ends'; also her individuality and the specialness of visits to her house: 'She was brown eggs … teapot'
Contrast	the noisy life force of Aunt Julia versus silence after she has died: 'silenced in the absolute black'
Enjambment	various examples such as 'pouring wetly/round house-ends' convey sense of her energy

Childhood memories

All the above points could be included here – as the impressions we form of Aunt Julia are based on MacCaig's childhood memories of her. To these add:

Technique	Effects
Word choice	'the only house …' emphasises how exciting/special it was to visit her; 'lain at night … absolute darkness … box bed': captures the intensity of childhood experience, strangeness of this unique location; 'crickets being friendly': disarms any feeing of threat by emphasising warmth and 'magical' proximity of nature
Alliteration	'box bed': conveys sense of fun, plaything, exciting

Adult regret about lack of communication

Again, some of the above points could be included here.

Technique	Effects
Structure	end of stanza 1: focus on inability to communicate; end of final stanza: returns to this idea, with 'questions/unanswered' ending on the word which sums up their inability to understand one another
Word choice	'answer … understand' in stanza 1: 'understand' develops/explains why he could not 'answer'; 'by the time I had … grave' shows his sad reflection on the futility of his attempt to communicate; 'learned/a little' shows how modest his grasp was – too little, too late; 'silenced … absolute black' emphasises the finality of her loss; echoes the 'absolute darkness' earlier; 'hear her still, welcoming me' shows her continuing importance in his life
Repetition	'I could not' in stanza 1, both emphasises his inability to connect with her and focuses on the word that changes/intensifies – 'answer' becomes 'understand'; 'getting angry, getting angry' shows building of frustration
Alliteration	'learned … little … lay' draws ideas together, highlighting his regret
Contrast	'very loud and very fast' versus 'silenced': A.J. as a life force contrasts with the silence of death; 'very loud and very fast' versus 'learned a little': her strength, energy and purpose contrasts with his ineffective efforts

Part two: exam-style analysis

Now that you know the poem really well, have a go at making up 'exam-style' questions on it. Aim for five questions: four of these should be on 'Aunt Julia' and the final question (**out of 8 marks if you are studying National 5 and 10 marks if you are studying Higher**) should ask about a link between this poem and at least one other of MacCaig's that you have studied. Try making up the 'Marking Instructions' too: this is a really good way of working out the kind of answers you will be expected to give in your exam. Then, swap with another group and try their questions. Later you can enjoy marking their efforts!

Part three: planning an essay

(There are examples of completed essays later in the book.)

Remember that you will only be writing a critical essay on MacCaig's poetry if you have studied more than one Scottish text/writer from the SQA list and have used your other writer/text for the 'Scottish text' part of the exam.

Critical Essay plans

Here is a critical essay question on poetry. Read it over carefully.

- Choose a poem which made a lasting impression on you. Explain briefly what the poem is about, then, by referring to appropriate techniques, show how the poem has made this lasting impression.

This kind of question could appear at either National 5 or Higher level.

In your group, you are going to plan how you would answer it.

There are different ways of planning this essay. Here are two basic plans:

Plan A

Begin with an introduction: identify the text and writer and begin to answer the question by rewording it. Briefly establish what the poem is about and why it has made such an impression on you (due to MacCaig's use of various techniques).

Work through the poem, starting at stanza 1. Identify the main ideas and explain how techniques are used to develop these, making a lasting impression on you. Show how the ideas build up towards the climax of the final stanza.

Conclusion: sum up the main points you have made in your essay.

Plan B

Begin with an introduction: identify the text and writer and begin to answer the question by rewording it. Briefly establish what the poem is about and why it has made such an impression on you (due to MacCaig's use of various techniques).

Work through the key ideas in the poem: Aunt Julia's personality; childhood memories; his adult sense of regret about their lack of communication. Explain each idea fully and show in detail how techniques are used to develop these, making a lasting impression on you.

Conclusion: sum up the main points you have made in your essay.

Task

Choose one of the basic plans above and, with a partner, create a more detailed version which includes details, examples and explanations.

Once you have planned your essay, swap with another group for some feedback. As an optional extra, write the essay you have planned. You should use your group plan to write your essay individually.

'Sounds of the Day'

This poem is very much an analysis of personal feelings, dealing perceptively with the emotions involved in an experience we can all understand: the break up of a relationship. It uses first-person narration (the speaker of the poem uses 'I') describing how he/she felt when the relationship ended. MacCaig has created an effective 'persona' – a character who speaks his words, not necessarily based on himself.

As the title suggests, the poem is (at least in the first half) dominated by techniques which create sound effects of various types, though there is also effective use of imagery, word choice, structure … techniques you are familiar with, from MacCaig's other poems. MacCaig winds these techniques tightly together in this short, complex, brilliant – and ultimately very painful and poignant – poem.

Questions

Read the poem quickly and consider the general questions that follow with a partner.

1. What does the title refer to?
2. What is the effect of using the direct address 'you' (stanza 3)?
3. Looking at the poem as a whole, what general point can we make about the contrast between sounds and silence?
4. Which two senses does MacCaig conjure up? One is easy, the other tricky – look at the final stanza.

Possible answers

1. These sounds are memories from a special day – 'the day', not just 'a day'. Maybe their final day together? Or just a day from happier times? In his original and creative way, MacCaig is going to focus on sounds that the speaker associates with happier times, rather than things seen.

2. The speaker is talking directly to the woman who has left him – so his account of the experience is all the more personal and powerful.

3. Sounds mean life, energy, amazing things going on around them (all linked to nature). So, silence means the opposite of this.

4. Hearing is the easy one (stanzas 1–3). Did you notice, also, the reference to touch (to be precise, numbness and pain) in stanza 4?

Now for some detailed analysis. Remember, sound is vital (though there are effective visual images too).

Some 'sound' techniques to watch out for

Technique	Definition	Example
Alliteration	repetition of sounds at start of words	cute kitten
Onomatopoeia	sound of word imitates its meaning	sizzle, whisper
Inner rhyme	rhyme within a line (possibly within words)	I fell down a well
Assonance	vowel sounds rhyme, but the consonants in the words do not	the pup was stuck
Half rhyme	not quite rhyming	the pillow is yellow

Textual explosion!

The first five lines have been exploded for you. Read over them and try to spot as many sound (and other effects) as you can in lines 6–9.

'Sounds of the Day'

> Alliteration/onomatopoeia

> **Assonance:** horses/ford
> **Half rhyme:** add 'crossing'

> **Alliteration:** crossing/creaked
> **Onomatopoeia:** creaked

> **Alliteration:** premises/private

> **Onomatopoeia** and **inner rhyme**

When a clatter came,
it was horses crossing the ford
When the air creaked, it was
a lapwing seeing us off the premises
of its private marsh. A snuffling puff
ten yards from the boat was the tide blocking and
unblocking a hole in the rock.
When the black drums rolled, it was water
falling sixty feet into itself.

Task

Discussion

What impression is MacCaig giving us of this important 'day'? Add imagery and subject matter (observation of nature) to your thoughts about sound. You might also like to think about the use of the pronoun 'us' and the sentence structure he uses.

Possible answers

Thoughts on stanza 1

In this stanza, natural description dealing with sounds, repetition of sentence structure and the use of metaphor ('black drums rolled') creates a definite 'pattern'. The whole idea of observing nature turns into a kind of witty 'game'. Importantly, it's a shared game ('us') and it shows real delight in the world of nature. This is there to be enjoyed and explored – and there are touches of humour in, for example, the 'lapwing seeing us off the premises' and the playful sounds of 'snuffling puff'. The various experiences of nature are linked by plentiful use of sound effects, often more than one in the same word or phrase, for example 'clatter came'. There is effective use of alliteration: 'crossing/ creaked'; inner rhymes and half rhymes: 'off/snuffling/puff', 'blocking/rock/black'. These sounds create an echoing effect, linking ideas together, suggesting an inner harmony in their relationship.

The repeated use of a specific sentence structure, beginning with a subordinate clause ('When ...') and moving on to the main clause ('... it was ...') reinforces the idea of a guessing game. First we are given the sound – and then the thing (horse, bird, tide, waterfall) causing the sound. (Having said that, the 'tide' one doesn't have 'when' at the start, but it is almost the same.) The little pause between sound and its cause helps to create a moment of suspense, between the 'puzzle' (what is causing that sound?) and the 'answer'.

Did you notice a slight change in tone in the final two lines of this stanza? The metaphor of the 'black drums' (for the waterfall sound) has an ominous feeling, as if something dramatic and unpleasant is about to happen.

Now look at stanzas 2 and 3 and try the TQE approach. You are becoming an expert at this now, so you've been given just a little help to start you off.

Technique (T)	Quotation (Q)	Effect (E)
Stanza 2, line 1 Structure	'When the door'	Focus on moment of door closing/dramatic
Stanza 2, line 2 Onomatopoeia		
Stanza 2, line 2 Word choice		
Stanza 2, lines 2–3 Enjambment		
Stanza 2, line 3 Word choice		
Stanza 3, line 1		Simple statement of hurt, betrayal
Stanza 3, line 2		Suggests lack of warmth, life
Stanza 3, line 2		Emphasises extent of sense of loss – universal

Stanzas 2 and 3 are devastatingly simple in their statement of loss: it is the end of everything for the speaker. How is this achieved?

Stanza 2 appears to continue the playful 'guessing game' of stanza 1, but, looking closely, we see that the game is over. There are no 'mystery sounds' in the 'When ...' part of the sentence, no metaphors – just the reality of the door shutting and what it implies. She's left him. Bleak sounds signal the end of joy ('scraped shut') and the finality of the change is conveyed in 'the end of all the sounds there are'. Nature, life, fun ... all these 'noisy' things are over for him.

Stanza 3 is very short, direct, poignant, with the reason for the change from sound to silence stated starkly: 'You left me.' The extreme quiet of the dying fire suggests loss of warmth, love, life. Note the use of enjambment in both of these stanzas to suggest the emotion which, though understated, is brimming over.

Now for the big finish!

Now on to the final stanza: we're used to a 'big finish' from MacCaig, using the final lines of the poem to push home the meaning, or provide a chilling twist. This poem is no exception.

Analysis

In pairs or in groups read the final stanza again: it concentrates on the feelings of the speaker, after being left by the person he loves.

Make a list under the following headings, noting how each technique contributes to conveying these feelings. You might like to do a couple by yourself and then get back together in your groups to compare notes. Remember that there will be some overlap, e.g. between imagery and word choice. Note also what is **not** there.

Word choice	Imagery	Line length and structure	Final line of the poem

Analysis summary

In stanza 4 there is no more sound imagery: that described happiness. To put across the feeling of inner numbness and sense of 'nothingness' MacCaig uses the corresponding physical sense: the central image of this stanza is the hand plunging into 'freezing water'. Let's see how that works:

Line 1 is dominated by the words 'hurt' and 'pride only'. This was his initial reaction: unpleasant, but not deeply wounding. This is the 'bangle of ice': a shock but not long-lasting. The short line 'forgetting that' focuses on his mistake: the reality of loss is going to be much more painful. Then the word 'plunge' to describe the hand entering the water: this suggests a strong and wholehearted submerging. Ironically, 'plunge' seems to suggest his total involvement in the relationship: the numbness seems to point to his inability to delight in the world any more, the feeling of something 'dead' within. The 'whole hand' echoes 'all the sounds there are': the totality and finality of the loss. The final word in the poem, after all the richly noisy description, so full of life, is 'numb'. Note that stanza 4 is all one sentence, building to the climax of that final word.

One final point about pronouns

Look carefully through the poem. Try to spot when MacCaig uses 'us', 'you', 'me' or 'I'.

For example:

- Stanza 1, line 4: 'a lapwing seeing **us** off the premises'. They are together, sharing this experience.
- Stanza 3, line 1: '**You** left **me**': 'us' has become 'you' and 'I'. They are separate now. And there is a definitely accusing tone in 'You left me'.
- Stanza 4, line 1: '**I** thought **I** was hurt in **my** pride only'. He is alone, with only his hurt feelings for company.
- Stanza 4, lines 3–5: '**you** … **your** hand … **you** feel … **your** wrist'. The 'you' here is the generalised form, used to mean 'anyone'. Is he afraid now to focus on his feelings at the end – trying to make it impersonal?

Task

With a partner or in a small group, try making up an exam-style group of questions on this poem. Remember that you need four (or thereabouts) shorter questions, out of 2, 3 or 4 marks. These should focus on the ideas of the poem and the techniques used to convey these to the reader. Start at stanza 1 and try to think of something you could ask on the key ideas and techniques through the poem. For your final question, think of a link with at least one other poem. This could be thematic (e.g. theme of relationships) or stylistic (e.g. building up to the 'big finish'.) Remember to make up 'Marking Instructions' too; this will really help you get to know the poem well. Try swapping your questions with another group and marking their efforts afterwards.

Task

Essay planning

(There are examples of completed essays later in the book.)

Have a go at planning this essay question, which (in one form of words or another) is the basis of many poetry essay questions at both National 5 and Higher levels.

Choose a poem which deals with an important subject effectively. Briefly explain what the subject is and, in detail, show how the poet uses poetic and language techniques to explore this subject.

First, think about what the question is asking you to do. You need to be clear, first of all, about the subject of the poem. In other words, what is the poem about? Then (and this will form most of your essay) you need to be able to analyse ('show how') techniques used to explore the subject.

'Sounds of the Day' is, clearly, about how painful it is to lose someone when a relationship ends. This is an 'important subject'. MacCaig makes use of a range of techniques to explore this subject, as you know.

Try, either with a partner or on your own, to plan an essay on this question.

On the next page is one way you could approach this essay question. (Remember that there is no one, definitely 'correct' way to write an essay like this. There are many valid approaches.) This is a much more detailed plan than the ones on 'Aunt Julia'. Read it carefully and compare it with your own. Don't worry if the plan you have created is much shorter – or deals with things in a slightly different order. Remember the importance of quoting as part of your analysis.

Possible essay plan

1. Introduction: introduce the poem and poet by rewording the question, e.g. 'A poem which deals with an important subject effectively is ...'. Do not start by saying 'I am going to write about ...' (the marker knows you are!). So, refer to the question and mention what the important subject is and how MacCaig uses a range of techniques to explore it.

2. 'Briefly explain what the subject is' – that means, in this case, probably one paragraph (or two, at most). Sum up the situation that the speaker describes in the poem, both before and after the relationship ended.

3. Now the major analysis part of your essay: 'in detail, show how the poet uses poetic and language techniques to explore this subject'. You could begin with structure of the poem: examine briefly the contrast between stanza 1 and the three shorter stanzas that make up the rest of the poem. You should comment on the differing emotions involved. This could mean commenting on the shift in tone and mentioning the changing types of metaphors and descriptions used – from those which capture the pleasure of listening to sounds – to those which describe the end of sound – through to the final sense of numbness (the climax of the poem).

4. Now look at stanza 1 in more detail. For example, the repetitive sentence structure ('When the ... it was ...') and what this suggests: the sense of nature as a 'game' which the speaker and partner have enjoyed together. You should examine the use of sound and imagery: quote and then explain/ analyse. You may not be able to cover every single example but should do enough to show the marker that you have confident understanding of the poem's techniques (perhaps three examples). You might want, here, to comment on use of first-person style, to create a sense of immediacy: mention 'us'.

5. Move on to stanzas two and three. Show how the pattern of stanza 1 seems to continue but in fact changes ('When the door ...') as a new tone is established: silence replaces sound. Discuss the symbolic significance of the door shutting. There is a natural link with the symbolism of the 'quietest fire'. This might be where you describe the use of other pronouns: 'us' changing to 'you' and 'I'.

6. The climax of the poem: stanza 4. The central image of the plunging hand into freezing water is vital here: remember to show how this technique (and others) is used to develop the important subject – the feeling of loss at the end of a relationship.

7. Conclusion: sum up the main points you have made. Keep your focus on how MacCaig makes effective use of the techniques you have discussed to convey the subject: the pain of a person in love who faces rejection and the emotional journey this involves.

To finish off your study of this poem, you could try writing the essay, using the plan above.

'Memorial'

The final poem in our MacCaig selection is a superbly crafted study of bereavement, the reaction to the death of a loved one. (A 'memorial' is something to remember someone by: think of a war memorial, to remember soldiers who have died.)

It is, of course, very moving and emotional – but completely unsentimental in its treatment of this highly charged subject. We see MacCaig at his most skilful in his creation of complex images and sound effects, which, along with word choice, repetition, use of tenses, enjambment, the structure of the poem (basically all the techniques you know well by now), work together to explore the major themes of the poem. These are the power of love, the impact of loss and the capacity of human beings to sacrifice and suffer.

Textual explosion!

As you are, by now, an expert on analysis of poetry, you are going to have a go at 'exploding' the whole text yourself – either with a partner or as an individual challenge. Here are some hints with techniques to get you started.

'Memorial'

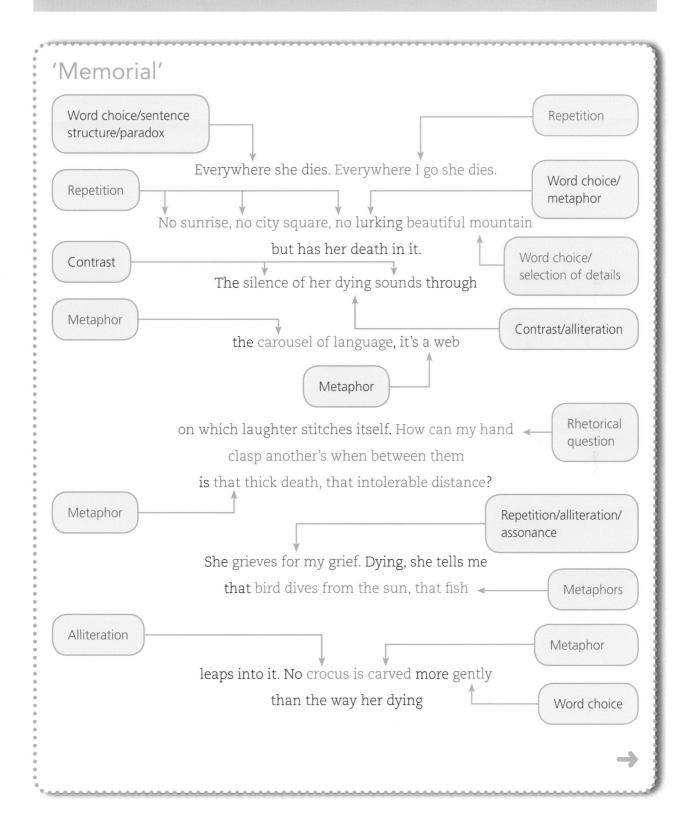

Word choice/sentence structure/paradox

Repetition

Repetition

Everywhere she dies. Everywhere I go she dies.

Word choice/ metaphor

No sunrise, no city square, no lurking beautiful mountain

Contrast

but has her death in it.

Word choice/ selection of details

The silence of her dying sounds through

Metaphor

Contrast/alliteration

the carousel of language, it's a web

Metaphor

on which laughter stitches itself. How can my hand

Rhetorical question

clasp another's when between them

is that thick death, that intolerable distance?

Metaphor

Repetition/alliteration/ assonance

She grieves for my grief. Dying, she tells me

that bird dives from the sun, that fish

Metaphors

Alliteration

Metaphor

leaps into it. No crocus is carved more gently

than the way her dying

Word choice

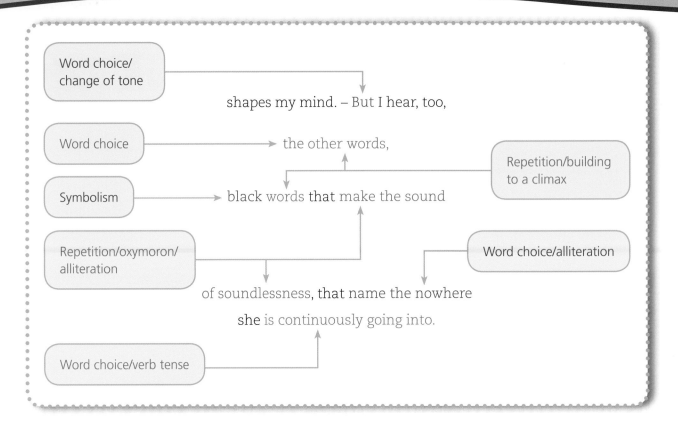

Word choice/
change of tone

shapes my mind. – But I hear, too,

Word choice

the other words,

Repetition/building
to a climax

Symbolism

black words that make the sound

Repetition/oxymoron/
alliteration

Word choice/alliteration

of soundlessness, that name the nowhere

she is continuously going into.

Word choice/verb tense

Task

Now try the final stanza (on the next page) without
any help.

Ever since she died

she can't stop dying. She makes me

her elegy. I am a walking masterpiece,

a true fiction

of the ugliness of death.

I am her sad music.

Questions

Now, with your partner, try to sum up:

1. What is the poem saying about loss of a loved one?
2. How does MacCaig use techniques effectively to explore this theme?

(There is a lot here: in an exam question – especially an essay – you would have to be selective.)

Possible answers

These notes are very detailed to help you prepare for both analysis and essay questions.

1. The main thing the poem is saying about this sort of loss is that, although the death has already happened, the sense of loss is still with the speaker, every single day. It is everywhere, in every activity, preventing normal interaction and relationships. Stanza 1 establishes this idea. Stanza 2 shifts perspective to the time before the death (though still described as if it is happening now) and the incredible heroism and love of the dying woman. She was most worried, not about herself, but about the loved one whom she knew she would be leaving behind (the speaker). We are told that she tried to 'soften' her own death for him, before it happened. However, no amount of anticipation could prepare him for the absolute bleakness of losing her. Stanza 3 reinforces these ideas through the speaker's description of himself as a living tribute to the woman who has gone.

2. The poem's opening, 'Everywhere she dies' hits us with dramatically simple **word choice** and **sentences structure**. It is a **paradox** – how can it make sense to say she dies 'everywhere'? The answer is, of course, that for him her death is everywhere: everything around him makes him think of it. This is reinforced by the **repetition** in, 'Everywhere I go she dies', with 'I go' pinning the idea to his personal experience of the world now. **Repetition** of 'no' in line 2 hammers home the fact that nothing remains untouched by her death: MacCaig gives a varied list of potentially exciting things to experience in the world, but none of them can really be enjoyed now – 'sunset ... city square ... lurking beautiful mountain'. Is there a sinister note in the metaphorical use of the word 'lurking'?

    The rest of stanza 1 develops the idea of her death being a part of everything, through the use of various techniques. The **contrast** between 'normal', alive things and the sense of her death comes across strongly, through **imagery** and **sound effects**. There is the **image of a carousel** to describe language/communication – a fairground ride full of life, sound, colour, movement – but there is a hushed 'silence' running through all attempts to communicate now. Note the **paradox** of 'silence of her dying sounds through' (highlighted by the 's' **alliteration**) – how can 'silence' sound through anything? But it does – it resounds through – and dominates – everything. The **metaphor** of the 'web' refers to weaving – a piece of woven cloth – which represents his awareness of her death. 'Laughter' – meaning feelings of joy – 'stitches itself' onto this web, but is awkward, out of place.

There are also sinister connotations of a spider's web – a trap. The final sentence of stanza 1 is a **rhetorical question**, raising the issue of how normal interaction (represented by the 'clasp' of a hand gesture of greeting, friendship, affection) can continue, when his thoughts of the death come between him and the rest of the world. (Answer: it can't.) Awareness of the death is described as an actual, physical barrier: 'that thick death, that intolerable distance'.

Stanza 2 continues the **complex interplay between images and sound**, focusing this time on the attempts of the dying woman to protect the speaker from the pain of her death. There is the (almost) **repetition** of 'grieves' and 'grief', with **alliteration** and **assonance** to tie the words together firmly. The stark word 'Dying' gives us the awful truth, but the way she explains it to him is full of beauty, of natural images: 'bird dives from the sun, that fish/leaps into it'. Death is presented as part of the natural cycle as these images conjure up a cinematic picture of the bird swooping down, against a golden background and the fish leaping up (heavenward?). The **metaphor** of the 'crocus ... carved ... gently' is particularly, brilliantly complex: the crocus is a spring flower, suggesting beauty and simplicity, a symbol of nature coming alive again. The idea of a 'crocus' being 'carved' conveys the idea that this humble but bright little flower has been created carefully, with love.

How does this relate to her death? The poem says, 'No crocus is carved more gently/than the way her dying/shapes my mind' – in other words, her dying message to him is as simple, life-affirming, gentle and beautiful as the crocus: death is natural, life goes on and he must try not to suffer too much. All that in fourteen words!

However, the word '– But' (and the dash that precedes it) introduces a change of **tone**. The rest of stanza 2 is dominated by **negative images and word choice**, conveying the terrible bleakness of the death itself, **contrasting** with those gentle and loving feelings beforehand. First, he mentions 'the other words' he hears, with 'the' suggesting that these are significant other words. Then, **repetition** plus **connotations** of mystery and shadows in 'black words'; the **paradox**, highlighted by **repetition** and **alliteration** in 'sound of soundlessness'; **alliteration** used to point towards 'nowhere' at the end of the line 'that name the nowhere'; and 'is continuously' to reinforce the never-ending nature of her death, his loss.

What does the build-up of all these techniques achieve? MacCaig conveys vividly the sense of nothingness, of death as the end of every positive thing. She is gone into 'nothingness' – there is no comforting sense of her presence still being with him (**contrast** with the first half of the stanza) – and she keeps on disappearing into nothing as he relives the horror over and over. We see again the **contrast** between sound representing life and silence meaning death/loss, as used in 'Sounds of the Day'.

Stanza 3 sums up his repeated experience of loss in the paradox: 'Ever since she died/she can't stop dying'. There follows a series of **metaphors** suggesting that his whole life is dominated by her memory, that he is a living tribute to her. They are **images of creativity**: 'walking masterpiece', 'true fiction' (also an **oxymoron**) and 'sad music', perhaps suggesting there is some solace in the act of artistic creation. The poem in itself, after all, is an example of this! Yet, there is a sinister **tone** in 'the ugliness of death' – these blunt, brutal words **contrast** with and undermine any sense of comfort in the ending.

Questions

National 5 exam-style questions

In pairs, answer the following questions.

1. By referring to two techniques in the opening stanza, show how the poet emphasises ways in which the world seems different now. **(4 marks)**
2. How does the final sentence of stanza 1 emphasise the narrator's confused state of mind? **(2 marks)**
3. In stanza 2, show how language is used to create a contrast in the narrator's reaction to her death. **(4 marks)**
4. How does stanza 3 indicate the change that he feels has come over him? **(2 marks)**

Final question

5. Show how MacCaig develops the theme of death in this and at least one other poem. **(8 marks)**

Possible answers

1. 'her dying' is seen as a 'web' **(1 mark)**

   Metaphor shows he is entrapped/overwhelmed by his loss **(1 mark)**

   Repetition of 'no' in line 2/repetition of 'everywhere' **(1 mark)**

   All familiar/life-enhancing things now remind him of her death **(1 mark)**

2. (Rhetorical) question **(1 mark)**

   Emphasises that normal ways of behaving and normal human interaction seem impossible/he does not know how to cope/move on **(1 mark)**

3. 'no crocus ... shapes my mind'/'bird dives from the sun'/'fish leaps into it' **(1 mark)**

   He feels her influence over him persisting despite her death/remembers her kindness in attempting to help him cope **(1 mark)**

   Contrast with: 'black words ... soundlessness' **(1 mark)**

   She has left a sense of absolute bleakness and loss **(1 mark)**

4. 'walking masterpiece'/'true fiction'/'I am her sad music' – metaphor **(1 mark)**

   He is transformed by her death/his life is dominated by it/he is a living tribute to her **(1 mark)**

5. Commonality: MacCaig presents death as a powerful, even overwhelming force in human relationships **(2 marks)**

   This text:

   - death is completely dominant, even over possible new/comforting relationships
   - death is ever present, never stops being experienced 'she can't stop dying'
   - death cuts the sufferer off from/defines reaction to all normal experiences

   Other texts:

   - 'Sounds of the Day': heartbreak through abandonment can be just as complete as death
   - 'Aunt Julia': lost opportunities in building relationship leaves feeling of regret after her death
   - 'Visiting Hour': fear of death dominates the senses/mind when visiting.

Questions

Higher exam-style questions

1. By referring to use of poetic technique, show how lines 1–3 provide an effective opening to the poem. **(2 marks)**
2. Show how MacCaig develops the theme of death in this and at least one other poem. **(10 marks)**

(**Note:** these are similar questions to National 5 but a different standard of answer is expected.)

Possible answers

1. Idea of utter devastation effectively introduced by techniques such as repetition ('Everywhere she dies', 'No') to convey the ubiquitous nature of his grief. Effective use of word choice: previously appreciated beautiful, exciting places and experiences ('No sunrise ... mountain') overshadowed by sense of her death.

   2 marks awarded for detailed/insightful comment plus reference; 1 mark for more basic comment plus reference; 0 marks for quote/reference alone.

2. **Up to 2 marks** can be achieved for identifying elements of commonality as identified in the question, i.e. MacCaig's development of theme of death.

   A **further 2 marks** can be achieved for reference to 'Memorial'.

   6 additional marks can be awarded for discussion of similar references to at least one other poem by MacCaig.

   In practice this means:

   * Identification of commonality **(up to 2 marks)** – theme of death

   From 'Memorial':

   * **Up to 2 marks** for comment on theme of death in 'Memorial'
     E.g. Overwhelming and constant nature of his grief, 'Everywhere she dies' – present tense shows he is still experiencing bereavement **(2 marks)**

   From at least one other poem by MacCaig:

   * as above (x3) for **up to 6 marks**

   OR

   * more detailed comment (x2) for **up to 6 marks**

   Thus, the final 6 marks can be gained by a combination of 3, 2 and 1 marks, depending on the level of depth/detail/insight. The aim would be to encourage quality of comment, rather than quantity of references.

Essay practice

Here is a selection of essay questions that you might choose to answer on the poem 'Memorial'.

With your partner, read them through. Which of them would you pick? Are there any you would avoid?

- Choose a poem which made a lasting impression on you. Explain briefly what the poem is about, then, by referring to appropriate techniques, show how the poem has made this lasting impression.
- Choose a poem in which the poet explores an important subject. Explain what the subject is and, by referring to appropriate techniques, show how the poet adds to your understanding of the subject.
- Choose a subject in which the poet creates a striking atmosphere or mood. Identify the mood or atmosphere and, by referring to appropriate techniques, show how the poet creates it effectively.

Pick one of the three questions above and plan and write an essay for it, using the notes on 'Memorial'.

For Higher level, here are some alternatives from the SQA specimen paper (available to download from SQA's website):

- Choose a poem in which the poet explores one of the following emotions: grief, happiness, love, alienation. Discuss how the poet's exploration of the emotion has deepened your understanding of it.
- Choose a poem which features a relationship. Discuss how the poet's presentation of this relationship adds to your understanding of the central concern(s) of the poem.

Making connections

Here are some links between the six Norman MacCaig poems you have studied (helpful for that final Scottish text question):

Thematic content	Poem(s)
Loss	'Memorial', 'Sounds of the Day', 'Visiting Hour', 'Aunt Julia'
The 'human condition'	'Assisi', 'Basking Shark', 'Memorial'
Incident prompting deeper thought	'Assisi', 'Basking Shark', 'Visiting Hour', 'Sounds of the Day'
A memorable person	'Aunt Julia', 'Assisi' and 'Memorial' (not major focus here but links could be made)
Emotional/upsetting/unsettling/significant experience	all of them
Makes you think about life	all of them
Memories	all of them
Sudden/unexpected encounters	'Basking Shark', 'Assisi'

Techniques	Poem(s)
Written from a particular standpoint	all of them
Contrast	all of them
Imagery	all of them – a particularly rich area in MacCaig's writing
Sound	all of them, particularly 'Sounds of the Day'
Structure	all of them – MacCaig specialises in 'the big finish'

CHAPTER 5
EXPERT COMMENTARIES

Anne Donovan (National 5)

Choose a novel or short story or a work of non-fiction in which you sympathise with one of the characters. By referring to appropriate techniques, show how the author has gained your sympathy for this character.

Sample essay

'Dear Santa' is a short story by Anne Donovan that concerns a central character who believes she is unloved by her parents. As such, the reader feels sympathy for her. The poem is told in first-person narrative mode from the girl's point of view and is written in Scots. The story deals with Alison's realisation that her childhood is ending and her reaction is to become jealous of her younger sister.

The opening statement provides a wonderful hook for the reader to encourage further exploration: 'Ma mammy disnae love me'. Immediately, sympathy is evoked from the reader as no child should feel like this. The reader needs to find out why the child would think this and so continues to read. The key to the way in which the reader is captured is the ironic contrast between the expectations established by the title and the actuality of the character's situation. The title makes us think of a child's letter to Santa asking for presents. The contrast between this expectation and the opening line is quite shocking for the reader.

The story is told in first-person narrative and written in Scots. This makes the piece more believable and makes the reader more sympathetic to character/narrator. This technique also involves the reader in the story as we hear only her view of the world. The use of the present tense also heightens the character's difficulty. This is something that is a problem now and needs to be solved urgently. As such, the girl's problems are given the weight of desperation.

Characterisation, too, helps to create sympathy for the main character. Alison's character is both complex yet realistic and we believe in her plight easily. Her awareness of her predicament is highlighted in word choices and imagery such as:

'and ah'm this big lurkin thing at the endy the back row, daurk and blurred'.

Here, we see Alison's view of herself. She is tall and clumsy as she is still developing and maturing. As she has yet to reach maturity, she is in a kind of limbo, not quite grown up and not quite a child any more, and so she shies away from people and her appearance is indistinct, 'daurk and blurred'. We, the readers recognise this as we have experienced it, to some degree, ourselves and we share in her awkwardness. →

To further highlight this, Donovan contrasts Alison with her younger sister to show why Alison felt jealous and why she could have felt that she was unloved. While Alison is told to be more like her sister and that she is 'big fur her age', Katie is praised for looking 'pure beautiful' and 'just lik an angel' with her blonde hair and prettiness. This merely serves to further emphasise Alison's already heightened sense of her own awkwardness as she is contrasted with her younger sister.

The setting of the story also contributes towards gaining sympathy for the central character. Christmas is a time for people, and especially children, to be happy. This makes Alison's situation even sadder and increases our sympathy for her. However, the setting allows the writer to show Alison's wishes and hopes in her attempts to write a letter to Santa 'Could you make ma mammy love me?' The 'dirty grey' sky mirrors the way Alison feels, whereas a white Christmas would have less effect on the reader because it would give a dream-like quality to Alison's Christmas.

The ending is very moving as the mother gives Alison hope that she loves her saying 'There's nothing wrang wi' broon hair', which, although it doesn't sound much, means more because the mother is not demonstrative like many Scottish people. Symbolically the mother leaves the door open slightly at the end letting 'a wee crack of light' fall across Alison's bed. As such, we see a ray of hope entering into Alison's life.

Donovan explores several themes in this story in terms of growing up and the awkwardness associated with it and also through exploration of the idea of favouritism in families. The last point raises many issues. Might we have felt similar to Alison? Does this really happen or is it just that we are very sensitive to how we are treated by our parents? Or is there just a little bit of favouritism in every family and we shouldn't worry too much about this?

In conclusion, 'Dear Santa' creates sympathy for its main character through the use of a variety of techniques.

Expert commentary

- Meets the demands for technical accuracy as the communication is very clear, is consistently accurate, with an effective structure dealing with key aspects of the story within paragraphs that are accurate and effective. (20–18)
- Understanding shows a high degree of familiarity and it is consistently relevant although there could have been more signposting to the keywords of the question throughout. (20–18, possibly sliding into 17–14)
- There is a thorough awareness of the writer's broad techniques and while quotation is used throughout the essay, this could have been strengthened. (20–18, sliding into 17–14)
- Commentary is very good. (20–18)

18/20

Edwin Morgan (National 5)

In the critical reading examination paper, you have 45 minutes to write a critical essay on a previously studied text from drama, prose, poetry, film and TV drama, or language study.

In the examination, you might choose to use your knowledge of Morgan's poetry to respond to **either** a textual analysis **or** a critical essay, but **not both using the same author**.

The sample answer below is 'exploded' to show you how it answers the critical essay question.

Task

Read the task and then the essay, in pairs. Then read the comments, in pairs. Finally, add **five** additional comments of your own that you think would strengthen the essay.

Question

Choose a poem which deals with an unusual theme. Show how the language used by the poet made the theme clear.

Sample essay

'Trio', by Edwin Morgan, appropriately, deals with three themes: religion, friendship and the fact that living life to the full can combat all the negative things that life has to throw at us.

- Poem and poet are named.
- The broad themes are mentioned first.
- The key theme is then given.

The poem's title, 'Trio', suggests a range of things: a musical trio, the mystical number three, or even the Holy Trinity of Father, Son and Holy Spirit in Christianity. The setting is then given – Buchanan Street in Glasgow and we are introduced to the main characters that constitute the trio, 'a young man … the girl on the inside … and the girl on the outside'.

- The title is significant in showing us the theme(s).
- Setting is the next aspect of the text to be dealt with by the poet.
- Characterisation follows setting.

Here, we are struck by two things. The sentence structure is unusual with the subject of the sentence, 'a young man and two girls' delayed until the second line. This emphasises their movement, 'coming up' Buchanan Street towards the narrator who observes their movements from a higher elevation. Second, their movements are fast; it is cold so they move, 'quickly' on this 'sharp evening'.

It is important to show how technique highlights meaning/theme/purpose in the poem.

The narrator goes on to describe what they are carrying and this is done through the use of repeated sentence structures with some variation:

Again, another key technique is unravelled to show its effect(s).

'The young man carries a new guitar in his arms, the girl on the inside carries a very young baby, and the girl on the outside carries a chihuahua.'

Each then bears a gift. This is also happening at 'Christmas' which makes us think of the journey of the Magi who travelled to Bethlehem to offer gifts for the newborn Christ. The gifts are completely unlike those brought by the Three Wise Men – gold, frankincense and myrrh. That there is a 'very young baby' among them reinforces the biblical associations. Their gifts are all simply what makes each of them happy – the guitar, the dog and the baby.

> Setting takes us into the technique of biblical allusion/reference. How does this work here?

So, they bear similarities to the Magi, but significant differences, too. The reason for their journey is unstated but the impression we get is that they are visiting a friend or relative at Christmas, which is a very common thing to do, although their 'gifts' are unlike the exotic gifts of the Magi.

> The technique of contrast is important in the poem.

The impression we receive of the characters is that they are happy. Their collective 'breath' is described through the metaphor of the 'cloud of happiness'. Their breathing has merged into one cloud, which could suggest the idea of Heaven as we often imagine it typified in this way.

> The technique is extended/developed.

The characters contrast strongly with the environment surrounding them. It is cold and by implication dark as it is an evening in deepest winter. They, however, generate warmth, colour, light and boisterous energy.

As they approach the narrator, s/he hears the 'boy' say: 'Wait till he sees this, but!' indicating that the characters are intending to visit a friend or perhaps a relative.

> They near the narrator at this point just as the boy imagines the response of the recipient of the gift. He can hardly contain his excitement. This is shown in the inversion of the normal word order with the word, 'but' left until the end of the line.

The focus then shifts to the 'gifts'. The chihuahua is incongruously dressed in 'Royal Stewart', the tartan of the Scottish kings. It is a bright, warm, vibrant colour. The humour of the scene is further developed in the simile comparing the dog's coat to a teapot-holder. Here, the 'high', is juxtaposed with the 'low' and the ordinary as both are equally important in the poet's eyes. Despite the incongruous dress, the dog is clearly loved.

The next 'gift' is the baby itself. It, too, is full of light matching the 'Christmas lights' of line two and contrasting with the darkness and coldness of the setting in general. Synecdoche is used here to show

➡

just how happy the baby is, to: 'All bright eyes and mouth'. Finally, in this section of the poem, a simile is used to compare the baby to 'favours' we might find in a wedding cake. Again, the impression is that the baby is loved.

The next movement is to the final 'gift' – the guitar, and its descriptions are very unusual. It 'swells' under its 'milky' plastic cover. This suggests that it is pregnant, full of life and vibrant. The 'milky' plastic cover, too, makes us think of the milk the baby will drink. The main idea here is of new life.

Morgan then makes reference to the very modern symbols of Christmas – tinsel and mistletoe. The latter symbolises fertility and illumination while the former is a bright decoration of Christmas trees.

> There is a range of symbols in this poem.

The poet then takes us from biblical references of the nativity to Greek mythology and specifically the tale of Orpheus, the Greek musician who could charm all things living and dead with his music. He used this power to rescue his wife, Eurydice, from Hell. This use of allusion creates the impression that the trio is very powerful and capable of defeating the 'vale of tears' which is a reference to Christian belief in the trials and tribulations of daily life.

> The story of Orpheus here helps us to understand the significance of the trio and its power according to Morgan.

The key theme of this work is unusual and the next line of the poem highlights it very well.

'Whether Christ is born, or is not born, you

Put paid to fate,'

The trio has the power to counter life's challenges and 'put paid to fate'.

This is very interesting, unusual and unexpected because the poem is set at Christmas, contains close references to the nativity, mimics the journey of the Magi, and yet its ultimate message is not Christian – it is simply that rejoicing in the simple things like friendship will see us through the dark times.

This thematic message is conveyed clearly at the close of the poem where Morgan begins to use regal, mythical and military imagery to carry his key theme and so fate is seen as a king forced into humiliating abdication. The monsters, not of myth and fairytale, but of the year, are the daily and weekly trials against which we have to struggle in our lives. These are not mentioned overtly, but we know what they are: money worries, debt, concern

> The main point is made. Technique, Quotation, Explanation.

for the future, sickness and so on ... These are the 'monsters of the year' – the things we battle all year long. In the face of such a trio and their camaraderie, these things are 'scattered' like an army in defeat as they are unable to 'bear this march of three'.

The final image with which we are left in the poem is of the trio guarding against the 'monsters of the year' with plain, simple laughter – an unusual theme indeed.

> Final link to the specifics of the question

Expert commentary

The response opens by pointing to the question – an unusual theme. In fact, it points out three and draws out the unusual aspect.

> The opening line should address the question directly.

The second paragraph begins with the title and explains how it refers to areas of content.

The third paragraph deals with the technique of sentence structure and shows a thorough awareness of the techniques.

> This is necessary to gain the highest category of mark.

There is then a nice link to the next paragraph – the gifts and the allusion to the Magi is explained. This is a good example of the writer's line of thought being clearly communicated. Indeed, the writer then goes on in the next paragraph to tease out the differences between the old and modern Magi thus giving a very well-developed commentary of what has been gained from the text.

> Again, this well-developed commentary keeps us firmly in the highest range.

In the next two paragraphs beginning, 'The characters' and 'As they approach,' we are given a combination of analysis and commentary, both of which are necessary in an effective critical essay.

> The balance between these is important.

The essay then continues the analysis by exploring the significance of the three gifts. The analysis is full in each case and the techniques used are examined in some detail.

> Again, we are firmly in the highest range.

Following this, the writer then goes on to explain the different references in the poem: biblical and Greek and then the focus turns to the question itself – the unusual theme.

This is followed in the penultimate paragraph by a very detailed account of precisely how the theme is unusual. If we missed this, then the writer makes absolutely certain of the relevance of the task by finishing the piece with another clear reference to the task.

> This also keeps us in the highest range. This is clearly a thorough answer and it is very precise.

- Technical accuracy is very good. (20–18)
- High degree of familiarity with very good understanding and consistently relevant. This is shown by consistent references to key words in the question such as, 'unusual'. (20–18)
- Thorough awareness of the writer's techniques through confident use of critical terms such as themes, characterisation, sentence structures and religious allusion. Techniques and their functions are very well explained and well chosen. (20–18)
- A very well-developed commentary. (20–18)

20/20

Norman MacCaig (National 5)

Question

Choose a poem which deals with an emotional experience. Briefly describe the experience and show how the poet uses language and literary techniques to convey the intensity of the emotional experience.

Sample essay

In the poem 'Visiting Hour', Norman MacCaig describes the upsetting personal experience of visiting a loved one in hospital. The poem begins as he walks along the hospital corridor, taking in the sights, sounds and smells of the hospital. He reaches her ward and, as he approaches her bed, sees how very weak and frail she is. He is very upset by the experience and pessimistic about her chances of recovery. Finally, he leaves, feeling depressed because she is so ill and they have not really been able to communicate during the visit. MacCaig conveys the intense pain of this experience through effective use of a range of poetic techniques.

MacCaig's skilful use of literary techniques draws the reader into his experience from the outset. In stanza 1, he uses the metaphor 'combs my nostrils' to describe the way the hospital smells seem to force themselves physically into his nose. He is uncomfortable in this strange environment, as shown by the unusual word choice 'as they go bobbing along' (meaning his nostrils) instead of 'as I go bobbing along'. It is as if his nose does not feel like a part of himself. This shows the discomfort, emotional as well as physical, which he is suffering. The discomfort is further emphasised by the description of 'green and yellow corridors', colours we associate with sickness.

→

In stanza 2, the speaker sees a figure on a trolley being taken into a lift, perhaps to surgery or another ward. However, he describes it as 'What seems a corpse', showing that his mind is dwelling on death. The fact that the trolley 'vanishes/heavenward' reinforces the idea that everything around him seems to relate to death and loss. The speaker's pain comes across particularly strongly in stanza 3 where the broken, disjointed phrases:

'I will not feel, I will not

feel, until

I have to'

show that he is desperately trying to keep his emotions under control. Clearly, he is feeling, very intensely, despite what he says. The repetition of 'I will not feel' emphasises the fact that he is trying to hold back the pain.

In stanza 4, the speaker observes all the bustle of the hospital, especially the nurses, who seem to rush around in all directions at once. He emphasises their busyness by reversing the normal word order in 'here and up and down and there' instead of 'here and there and up and down'. He is also amazed by their cool, detached way of dealing with the day-to-day tragedies they have to face. Repetition in 'so much pain, so many deaths … so many farewells' emphasises this, as does the word choice of 'slender waists' and 'clear eyes', while 'miraculously' echoes back to the 'heavenward' of stanza 2. Their self-controlled professionalism, which he admires, contrasts strongly with his own feeling of pain and misery.

There follows the dramatic announcement at the opening of stanza 5 that he has reached his destination: 'Ward 7'. These two words are sudden and blunt, with the number '7' used to reinforce the sense that he has, perhaps, just seen the sign on the wall. It could be that he is dreading the visit so much that he feels he has arrived too quickly. MacCaig uses the metaphor 'white cave of forgetfulness' to describe where the patient is. True, she is lying in a white bed, with hospital linen and pillows, but the 'cave' idea also suggests that she is lying in a deep place which the speaker cannot reach. This is further emphasised by his mention of the 'distance of pain' between them. Even when standing next to her, he cannot quite reach her: he can sympathise with her pain but not feel it, just as she cannot really appreciate his presence because she is so ill. Further effective metaphors are used, such as the woman's arm being compared to a 'stalk', so thin and weak that it can hardly support the 'withered hand'. Here she is compared to a dying plant, withering away. A surprising image is used in 'a glass fang', the hospital drip sustaining her life, when we would normally associate a 'fang' with vampires, draining life away from their victims. MacCaig makes sure that we notice this unusual idea by adding alliteration in 'not guzzling but giving'. She is alive, possibly even awake, as her 'eyes move' but she is so weak that she cannot open them properly.

In the final stanza the speaker tries to understand the situation from the patient's point of view. He begins with 'She smiles a little' which perhaps suggests an awareness and appreciation of his visit. Yet this is followed quickly by a description of himself as a mere 'black figure'. This word choice suggests that, after all, she may not even recognise him. The words 'black figure' have connotations of the arrival of death, come to claim this very ill woman. As the bell sounds for the end of visiting hour, he imagines how she 'sees' him going away 'dizzily … growing fainter' as her illness and exhaustion mean that she is not quite alert or aware of things around her.

→

The final lines of the poem have a deeply sad, pessimistic tone. As he goes away, he is aware of how pointless the gifts are that he has left her. The word choice of 'books that will not be read' shows this, and especially the final words 'fruitless fruits'. This is a pun, as 'fruitless' can mean 'pointless', but the fruits are also 'fruitless' in that, for her, they have no taste or enjoyment: she is too ill to enjoy them. The speaker's final feeling, then, is of the sheer pointlessness of such a visit as the person he loves is too ill to be cheered or helped by it: she seems beyond help.

In conclusion, 'Visiting Hour' is an emotional and very effectively written poem in which MacCaig describes the intensely uncomfortable and unhappy experience of visiting a loved one in hospital. He manages to convey universally understood feelings vividly by using a range of literary techniques which combine to reveal to us how painful this experience is.

Expert commentary

The response on the poem 'Visiting Hour' by Norman MacCaig begins by addressing the 'Briefly describe the experience' part of the question. The experience of visiting a seriously ill loved one is identified and the emotional pain felt by the speaker is outlined.

The essay then deals with the poem chronologically, beginning with stanza 1. This, the main body of the essay, deals with 'language and literary techniques' used by the poet 'to convey the intensity of the emotional experience'. These comments are detailed and thoughtful, with many accurate observations on, for example, use of metaphors, word choice, repetition, tone and structure. The candidate has approached the question in a methodical way, with each paragraph focusing on specific techniques and their effects, linking these to the central question of how the emotional experience is conveyed.

Technical accuracy:

Very clear communication and effective structure.

Familiarity:

High degree of familiarity is shown and very good understanding of the central concerns of the text. Consistently relevant line of thought: the essay sticks well to the demands of the question.

Analysis:

Thorough awareness of the writer's techniques is shown and the candidate is confident when handling technical terminology. There is a very detailed and thoughtful explanation of stylistic devices, supported by quotations.

Evaluation:

Very well-developed commentary of what has been gained by the text. Candidate has clearly, genuinely engaged with the poem.

Summary:

Thorough and precise – very good.

20/20

Iain Crichton Smith (National 5)

Question

Choose a novel or short story which explores an important theme. By referring to appropriate techniques, show how the author has explored the theme.

Sample essay

'The Painter' by Iain Crichton Smith is a short story that explores an important theme: individuality versus conformity to those around us. Set in a small community, the story gives an account of the relationship between a boy, William Murray (the 'painter' of the title) and the people of the village where he and his mother live. William's individuality, expressed through his paintings, is accepted – even praised – until he makes the mistake of painting the ugly side of his neighbours. When he paints a violent incident and the villagers' enjoyment of it, he is attacked and his painting destroyed. Crichton Smith reveals the powerful pressure to conform through his depiction of William and the community which rejects him.

One technique used by Crichton Smith to develop this theme is the narrative style of the story. It is a first person narrative, told by the villager who destroys William's painting at the end. Interestingly, his name is never revealed and he tends to use the word 'we' when expressing his views. This is effective because it allows Crichton Smith to reveal the attitudes of the village, through the words of the narrator. It is through his eyes that we see William's crucial 'offence' – painting the brutal fight and the faces of the villagers during the violence. He is forcing them to 'see' their true selves, 'the varying expressions of lust and happiness', not the self-satisfied picture of decent respectability they like to believe in. Significantly, looking back on the incident, the narrator comments, 'I have never regretted what I did that day': he has learned nothing from it. He still sees William as the one who is wrong, the one who refused to conform.

Through this narrator, we are given glimpses of William Murray himself. For example, he describes William as dressing 'in a very slapdash manner' and we can tell that the boy's slightly bohemian style does not meet with the narrator's approval. William's delicate beauty and quiet, 'strange' personality seems out of place in the rough, physically hard world of the crofting community. Nonetheless, at first he finds his niche through painting pictures of, for example, the villagers' dogs. While praising the accuracy of some of his paintings, they are less keen on ones which contain strange or disturbing images – the more artistic ones – when he 'made our village less glamorous on the whole than we would have liked'. So, Crichton Smith hints earlier in the story that William does not quite fit in, preparing us for the dramatic rejection at the end.

Crichton Smith further develops the theme by the comparison between William's offence and that of another villager, 'Red Roderick', the man who causes the fight at the end. Roderick, we are told, although hardworking and a good family man when sober, becomes violent when drunk. He is also bitter and resentful towards his father-in-law, who has inconveniently lived longer than expected, preventing Roderick from inheriting money through his wife. Towards the end of the story, Roderick – drunk – confronts his father-in-law and a violent scene follows, with both men swinging scythes at each other. It is this fight that the villagers gather to watch and that William captures in his painting. It is interesting to note that Roderick, despite his drunkenness and violence towards his family and others, is criticised but ultimately accepted, whereas William is rejected and shunned. We are left wondering why Roderick can be forgiven but William cannot. The crucial difference is that Roderick's behaviour does not challenge the community's view of itself: he does not 'stand outside' the community, observing and recording what he sees. William commits no acts of violence against individuals, but a greater 'crime' against the community. We see here how difficult it is to be an individual in a society which accepts violence more than criticism of itself.

The structure of the story helps to convey the theme, as it builds up to the climax where William's individuality, in the form of his creative activity, clashes with the 'rules' of the community to conform. During the fight between Red Roderick and his father-in-law, the narrator, who has gathered with the rest of the village to watch, notices William calmly painting the scene. Unlike the others, William is not caught up in the guilty excitement of the fight: he is observing and painting, not just the combatants but, crucially, the reactions of the villagers. Realising this makes the narrator lose control and Crichton Smith makes his fury clear by using effective language to describe William's observation, 'as indifferent to the outcome as a hawk's might be,' and his own reaction, 'the most bitter disgust'. The intensity of the narrator's feelings comes from a fear of having to face the truth about himself and his community. He did not want to see what he looked like when in the grip of the frenzied excitement that dominated them all during the fight. Not only the painting, but the boy himself is attacked in this confrontation between individuality (represented by William) and the narrator (representing conformity). The impact of this conflict is devastating for William and his mother, who are completely rejected by the village – they even destroy his other paintings, which – earlier – they had been proud of. Crichton Smith reveals here the dangers of being a creative individual in a world where conformity is essential to survive.

In conclusion, Crichton Smith explores the theme of individuality and conformity in this story. Through narrative style, characterisation, structure and style, he has created an effective piece which reveals how difficult and dangerous it can be to challenge the norms of the community to which we belong. Even something as apparently harmless as a painting can stir up feelings of fury and hatred against those who, like William Murray, express themselves without giving in to the pressures of conformity.

Expert commentary

The response begins by identifying the theme explored by the short story: individuality versus conformity. There is a brief introduction to the story and the main area to be explored, the contrasting depiction of William and the community, is outlined.

The essay then deals with a variety of specific techniques used to develop the central theme. This is a methodical approach which allows the candidate to select evidence from different parts of the text without slipping into retelling the story. The techniques include first person narrative, description of the painter himself, comparison with another character (Red Roderick), the structure of the story – building to a climax – and the language used in the climactic moments. The comments are perceptive and accurate, with a firm focus on the demands of the question. Quotations and references are used as appropriate.

Technical accuracy:

Very clear communication and effective structure.

Familiarity:

High degree of familiarity is shown and very good understanding of the central concerns of the text. Consistently relevant line of thought: there is a clear focus throughout the essay on the theme of individuality versus conformity.

Analysis:

Thorough awareness of the writer's techniques is shown and the candidate is confident when handling technical terminology. There is a very detailed and thoughtful explanation of stylistic devices, dealt with in a clear and methodical way, and quotations/references support these comments.

Evaluation:

Very well-developed commentary of what has been gained by the text. Candidate clearly understands the central theme of the story.

Summary:

Thorough and precise – very good.

20/20

The next two examples are Higher-style essay questions (though they are similar to National 5-style questions). These essays have been assessed according to the Higher Critical Essay Criteria.

Norman MacCaig (Higher)

Question

Choose a poem which conveys a strong message. Identify the message and, by referring to appropriate techniques, show how the poet leads you to a deeper understanding of the message.

Sample essay

In the poem 'Assisi', Norman MacCaig transforms personal experience to convey a message strongly critical of various types of hypocrisy and insensitivity. The poem uses the description of a visit to the ornate church of St Francis in Assisi, where a disabled beggar is sitting, neglected by the tourists and priest who pass him by, to show us how the humblest of human beings must be more highly valued than any amount of art or legends. In order to express this idea, MacCaig creates sympathy for the beggar (and others like him) and satirises the priest and tourists, before shaking us, the readers, out of our complacency.

The poem begins with a contrast between the beggar's pathetic imperfection and the magnificence of the three-tiered cathedral and the glorious reputation of its saint. At this point, MacCaig encourages us to feel pity (rather than empathy) for the beggar: the description objectifies him through the slightly 'distancing' implied metaphor of an abandoned puppet, sitting with its strings cut. His weakness and vulnerability are stressed, through words such as 'sat, slumped like a half-filled sack', with the alliteration tying together the meaning of the simile. There is a strong suggestion of lethargy and lack of fulfilment in 'half-filled' and he has 'tiny, twisted legs' which, because both 'tiny' and 'twisted', could not possibly support him in basic activities such as walking. Interestingly, the word 'tiny' is a diminutive term with non-threatening connotations. This initial description evokes a detached sympathy, rather than creating a strong sense of the man's humanity.

The contrast turns on one centrally positioned word: 'outside'. The unavoidable assumption is that he is outside the Church's concern as well as literally outside the building. This suggestion is built up through the obvious irony of St Francis as 'brother of the poor' being honoured by a glorious cathedral, while a beggar sits, ignored, outside. We are forced to ask if St Francis' ideals are actually being honoured. Though MacCaig appears to be simply giving the facts about St Francis' fame and reputation, the sight of the beggar makes them seem trivial and hollow. He was a 'talker with birds' – but what value has that, compared with the suffering of a human being? The stanza ends with a statement involving unusual word choice and syntax:

'over whom he had the advantage

of not being dead yet'

Saying he is 'not dead yet', rather than 'alive' suggests that he is merely existing, rather than truly living – and the comparison we draw with St Francis is that a dead man is being honoured while a living man is left to suffer. →

In stanza 2, MacCaig focuses on the priest, representative of the establishment whose priorities are being questioned. MacCaig has chosen his words carefully to show how spiritually empty he feels the priest's message to be. Words like 'clever' and 'stories' suggest that the description of Giotto's paintings is superficial and dishonest. The tourists are told that these paintings demonstrate 'the goodness of God' and 'the suffering of His son'. The smooth rhythm of these phrases, and the fact that the priest seems oblivious to the suffering outside, makes them seem glib, unthinking and meaningless. They might sound good and the paintings might look impressive, but they are empty. Coupled with the rhythm, the use of alliteration in 'goodness of God' and 'suffering of his Son' creates a slogan-like effect, as if they are phrases used in advertising. This again clearly indicates MacCaig's view that any spiritual message has been debased to the level of a sales technique.

To MacCaig, the paintings cannot reveal a 'goodness' which is absent in the world around him. He appreciates the artiness of the frescoes but not their message. This is implied in the last three lines when he pointedly refers to understanding the 'explanation and the cleverness' but not what is supposed to be the whole point of them, namely demonstrating God's goodness. It is what is omitted that shows us how he feels, a subtle form of irony. However, he keeps the omitted word ringing in our minds. 'Goodness' is echoed in 'understood' and 'cleverness'. It is important that all three words end their lines, giving the sounds a chance to 'draw together'. We can also see how the word 'goodness' is visually emphasised by ending such a long line: we notice it sticking out; then we notice it left out. The one idea omitted by MacCaig is thus put into our minds even as he rejects it. The message of the frescoes is undermined by the evidence of suffering around him. This is reinforced further by the use of childish words like 'clever' and 'stories' which suggest that the tourists are being deceived as easily as if they were children.

The tourists become the major focus of satirical criticism in stanza 3, in which MacCaig uses the extended metaphor of a group of chickens, suggesting that they are mindlessly and thoughtlessly 'swallowing' all they are told by the priest. The criticism is intensified by use of the phrase 'grain of the Word' to describe the priest's utterances. This is a reference, from the biblical parable of the Sower, of the power of God's truth to take root and grow in people's minds. Here, though, the empty words are gobbled up by people whose minds seem closed to reality and suffering. How can they be contented, having passed by the poor man outside?

As the poem builds to its climax, the message it conveys emerges even more strongly. It is here that the true power of the poem can be seen as MacCaig pulls away our complacency, forcing us to examine our own attitudes to those less fortunate. First, he emphasises the dignity and human worth of the man by using the metaphor 'ruined temple', which also neatly contrasts with the magnificent cathedral mentioned in stanza 1. He may be 'ruined' but he is also a 'temple', implying a spirituality more valuable than the artwork for which he is being neglected. We wonder how the tourists could have so callously passed and ignored him.

Then we find out why – in a description in which the horror and power are matched: 'whose eyes wept pus, whose back was higher than his head, whose lopsided mouth …' He is hideous: this time, we are not distanced from his monstrous appearance (as in stanza 1); it is thrust in our faces. We cringe inwardly and are as guilty in our revulsion as the tourists and the priest. MacCaig forces the beggar's grotesqueness upon us by insistent repetition of the clause structure beginning with 'whose …'. Suddenly the pattern is broken by the totally unexpected word 'Grazie', said by the beggar, as someone (perhaps the speaker) gives him money. To deepen our guilt, MacCaig continues to emphasise the inner beauty of the man, in contrast to his outer ugliness. His gratitude (in a world where he has very little to be grateful for) combines with the childlike sweetness of his voice and character, through the use of similes comparing him to a child (talking to her mother) or a bird (talking to St Francis) – innocent and loving images. The implication is that, to find such purity of life in someone with his problems is a miracle equal to St Francis' bird conversations. This man, with his beautiful nature and simple appreciation of life, along with his lovely attitude to other people, is a truer embodiment of Christian – or human – virtues than any amount of artwork or stonework, no matter how beautiful. He is a more fitting tribute to the life and values of St Francis. The fact that we, along with other representatives of humanity in the poem, failed to see this, distracted by his hideous appearance, conveys a powerful, chilling – and unexpected – message about our attitudes to others.

To conclude, in the poem 'Assisi', MacCaig presents a powerful criticism of our tendency to deny or turn away from the uncomfortable truth about our attitudes to the suffering of others. Through effective use of a range of poetic techniques, he not only satirises Church and society, represented by the priest and tourists, but forces us, the readers, out of our complacency into a recognition that we are no better.

Expert commentary

The response begins by identifying and explaining the message of the poem 'Assisi' by Norman MacCaig and outlines, in general terms, how MacCaig conveys the poem's central theme, through creating sympathy for the beggar, criticising other figures in the poem and, finally, attacking the complacency of the reader.

The essay then progresses through the poem's stanzas, exploring how MacCaig uses various poetic techniques to lead the reader 'to a deeper understanding of the message'. Fluent linking and the careful development of a coherent argument (leading to a climax) prevent this approach from becoming too 'mechanical'. Thus the candidate analyses MacCaig's use of, for example, contrast, imagery, sound effects, word choice, rhythm and structure – of lines, stanzas and the whole poem. Perceptive and detailed comments are made throughout the essay, revealing the candidate's genuine engagement with the poem and understanding of its theme and the techniques used to convey this.

Knowledge and understanding:

Comprehensive knowledge shown of the text. Relevant and coherent argument supported by selection of textual references.

Analysis:

Comprehensive analysis of the effect of features of language techniques.

Evaluation:

A committed, very clear evaluative stance with respect to the text and task.

Technical accuracy:

Few errors.

Meaning clear at first reading.

20/20

Iain Crichton Smith (Higher)

Question

Choose a short story in which a specific location or setting is crucial to the plot. Discuss how the writer makes you aware of the setting's importance and how this feature is used to enhance your appreciation of the text as a whole.

Sample essay

In the short story 'The Red Door' by Iain Crichton Smith, the setting of the small island community is crucial to the plot. The story concerns one morning in the life of Murdo, an island crofter, who wakes up to find his front door has been, mysteriously, painted red. His reaction to this small but highly significant occurrence – and his awareness of what the reaction of the rest of the community will be – forms the basis of the story. The setting – not just the physical environment of the village itself, but the collective opinion of the people living there – is not merely a background to character and theme, but forms an integral part of their development, enhancing the reader's appreciation of the text.

Crichton Smith makes us immediately aware of the setting's importance by placing Murdo firmly in the village environment from the outset. The story takes place just outside his front door, with the village and its conventions all around him. Murdo is presented to us as a self-sufficient character, unmarried and on pleasant – though not intimate – terms with his neighbours 'since he didn't offend anyone by gossiping'. He is 'liked' by omission, through not annoying others, rather than with any real shared affection. Even at this early stage, though, Crichton Smith hints that something in Murdo goes beyond the village conventions. His first action is to go 'into the cold air to see whether anything was stirring in the world around him', suggesting a questing after excitement, albeit in a modest way.

Murdo's newly transformed red door stands out: no one has ever had one before. Its brightness singles Murdo out in an environment where conformity is far preferred to individuality. Murdo has lived in the village all his life, like his parents before him. All the people he knows and any possibility of romance are centred in this community: it has, indeed, shaped him and, we would expect, defines his attitudes. Yet he finds himself examining his feelings about the door and, through this, realising that he is different from the community norm. His self-examination provides the tension in the story leading to the climax and resolution – not just of the 'door issue' but of his whole approach to life. His epiphany when faced with the red door frees him to knock on the door of opportunity, or, more specifically, of Mary, a free spirit, with whom he has a possibility of real happiness, not the passive version he has experienced so far.

Crichton Smith makes us aware of the environment's power to damage in the way that Murdo has been influenced by the all-pervasive nature of community opinion from childhood. To do anything individual or different is to court criticism or, worse, scorn. One example of this is the revealing incident when Murdo, 'a serious child who found it difficult to talk to children even of his own age' made the mistake of drawing attention to himself. Significantly, it was an overhead plane, symbol of travel and adventure 'beyond', which prompted him to exclaim, 'Thee, an aeroplane'. His lisping voice was mocked

➡

and he was dismissed as foolish. This, the only time he ever showed 'enthusiasm', brought down the derision of his peers on him: an already shy and serious boy, his social fate was sealed and he never grew in confidence. Later experiences undermined him further; clumsiness at sport, limited maths skills, inability to hold down a practical job on a fishing boat. He never excelled in the areas deemed desirable. As an adult, he supported his ailing parents by farming 'in a dull concentrated manner': there is a degree of competence, but no joy in this way of life. The lack of excitement is shown in Crichton Smith's depiction of Murdo at work: the sunlight may be 'sparkling from the blade' of his scythe, but Murdo, unaffected, is 'squat and dull'. Even love is determined by the limited possibilities of village life. We are told that Murdo's one attempt at romance was with a spinster (unnamed in the story, suggesting her lack of genuine, individual significance) who lived opposite him with her 'grossly religious mother'. We can see the overbearing nature of the island's version of Christianity in these words. The fact that her 'ferocious' cooking put him off suggests a lack of real connection between them and she is not described as a person, unlike the more spirited Mary.

Murdo's potential for character development and fulfilment is presented through his reaction to the door and, crucially, his separateness from the rest of the community's views. In this world of conformity to social expectations – doing the job his father did, living in the place his parents did, going to church because others do – the appearance of the red door seems to jolt Murdo out of a semi-conscious state. He realises that the red door has changed something about the village – and, significantly, himself. As Crichton Smith puts it: '"I have never," he thought with wonder, "been myself."' Immediately, the language used to describe everyday things begins to take on a magic: a crowing cock is 'belligerent and heraldic, its red claws sunk into the earth, its metallic breast oriental and strange.' The colour of the door, like the cock's claws, of course has symbolic significance. Murdo connects it with wine and blood: both dangerous; both evoking a sense of passion and life lived fully. Seeing the door not only prompts Murdo to contrast his own reaction – a sort of bewildered admiration – with the likely reaction from others (anger and pressure on him to paint it back). It also stirs something in him: a longing to have someone to love. A longing to live.

The personality of Mary is crucial in Murdo's evolution. The fact that he is drawn increasingly to her as he gazes at the door is significant. She habitually commits acts of 'rebellion' against the community – reading books, refusing to gossip, demonstrating artistic talent, taking solitary night time walks – and outbursts of genuine emotion, even if inconvenient. Murdo's climactic decision to knock on Mary's door is, thus, inspired by the courageous statement of his own. It is different; she is different: he, too, can be different. With a sudden thrilling moment of shock, he realises that he could leave the village, if they will not accept his new door – and his new identity. Crichton Smith conveys Murdo's fresh sense of the possibilities of life through references to childhood Christmases: the anticipation he feels now is reminiscent of 'stealing barefooted over the cold red [red again!] linoleum to the stocking hanging at the chimney'. As Murdo walks towards Mary's house, the world is imbued with a new magic in the 'sparkling frost' whose 'virginal new diamonds glittered around him, millions of them'.

In conclusion, setting is not just a backdrop to the story of 'The Red Door', but drives forward narrative, character and thematic development. Through Murdo's quiet struggle against the conformity he sees around him and has accepted throughout his life, Crichton Smith makes a clear statement about the human need for self-expression and individual fulfilment.

Expert commentary

This response begins by identifying the specific setting which will be explored in the essay: a small island community. The candidate points out that the setting does not just mean the physical environment but also means the collective opinion of the people living there – and it is this aspect of 'setting' on which the essay focuses. The introduction outlines the importance of this setting, not as a background, but as a vital element in development of character and theme.

The essay then examines the effect of this setting on the development of the main character, Murdo, and, through him, the theme of individual fulfilment in a conformist society. Various aspects of the story are considered: first impressions of Murdo; his initial reaction to the appearance of the red door, contrasted with the probable reaction of the village; the environment as a negative influence throughout his life; the transforming effect of the door on Murdo's attitudes; and the importance of the character of Mary. The candidate provides detailed evidence, with quotations as appropriate, and there is perceptive analysis of language used, for example, in the climax of the story. The candidate has clearly understood the story's central theme and how Crichton Smith uses techniques to develop this. It is a confident response to the question.

Knowledge and understanding:

Comprehensive knowledge shown of the text. Relevant and coherent argument supported by selection of textual references.

Analysis:

Comprehensive analysis of the effect of features of language techniques.

Evaluation:

A committed, very clear evaluative stance with respect to the text and task.

Technical accuracy:

Few errors.

Meaning clear at first reading.

20/20

APPENDIX
CRITICAL ESSAY MARKING GRIDS

National 5

Marks	20–18	17–14	13–10	9–5	4–0
The candidate demonstrates:	• **a high degree of familiarity** with the text as a whole • **very good understanding** of the central concerns of the text • a line of thought which is **consistently relevant** to the task	• **familiarity** with the text as a whole • **good understanding** of the central concerns of the text • a line of thought which is **relevant** to the task, although there may be some disproportion in parts of the essay	• **generally sound familiarity** with the text as a whole • **some understanding** of the central concerns of the text • a line of thought which is **mostly relevant** to the task	• **some familiarity** with **some aspects** of the text • **attempts** a line of thought but this **is not always maintained**	Although such essays should be rare, in this category, the candidate's essay will demonstrate one or more of the following: • it contains numerous errors in spelling/grammar/ punctuation/ sentence construction/ paragraphing • knowledge and understanding of the text(s) are not used to answer the question • any analysis and evaluation attempted unconvincing • the answer is simply too thin
Analysis of the text demonstrates:	• **thorough awareness** of the writer's techniques through analysis, making **confident** use of critical terminology • **very detailed/ thoughtful** explanation of stylistic devices supported by **a range of well-chosen** references and/or quotations	• **sound awareness** of the writer's techniques through analysis, making **good** use of critical terminology • **detailed** explanation of stylistic devices supported by **appropriate** references and/or quotation	• **an awareness** of the writer's techniques through analysis, making **some** use of critical terminology • explanation of stylistic devices supported by **some appropriate** reference and/or quotation	• **some awareness** of **the more obvious** techniques used by the writer through **explanation** • **attempts to use** critical terminology • **description** of **some** stylistic devices followed by some reference and/or quotation	

National 5 (continued)

Marks	20–18	17–14	13–10	9–5	4–0
Evaluation of the text is shown through:	• a **very well developed** commentary of what has been enjoyed/gained from the text(s), supported by **a range of** well-chosen references to its **relevant** features	• a **well developed** commentary of what has been enjoyed/gained from the text(s), supported by **appropriate** reference to its **relevant** features	• **generally sound** commentary of what has been enjoyed/gained from the text(s), supported by **some appropriate** references to its features	• **brief** commentary of what has been enjoyed/gained from the text(s), followed by **brief** reference to its features	
The candidate:	• uses language to communicate a line of thought **very clearly** • uses spelling, grammar, sentence construction and punctuation which are consistently accurate • structures the essay **effectively** to **enhance** the meaning/purpose • uses paragraphing which is **accurate and effective**	• uses language to communicate a line of thought **clearly** • uses spelling, grammar, sentence structure and punctuation which are **sufficiently** accurate • structures the essay **very well** • uses paragraphing which is **accurate**	• uses language to communicate a line of thought **at first reading** • uses spelling, grammar, sentence structure and punctuation which are **mainly** accurate • attempts to structure the essay **in an appropriate way** • uses paragraphing which is **mainly accurate**	• uses language to communicate a line of thought which may be disorganised and/or difficult to follow • makes some errors in spelling/grammar/ punctuation/ sentence construction • has not structured the essay well • has made some errors in paragraphing	

Higher

Marks	20–19	18–16	15–13	12–10	9–6	5–1	0
Knowledge and understanding **The critical essay demonstrates:**	• a comprehensive knowledge and understanding of the text • a comprehensive selection of textual evidence to support a relevant and coherent argument	• a very clear knowledge and understanding of the text • very clear textual evidence to support an argument which is clearly focused on the demands of the question	• a clear knowledge and understanding of the text • clear textual understanding to support the demands of the question	• an adequate knowledge and understanding of the text • adequate textual evidence to support a line of thought which has some focus on the question	• limited evidence of knowledge and understanding of the text • limited textual evidence to support focus on the demands of the question	• little knowledge and understanding of the text • little textual evidence to support focus on the demands of the question	
Analysis **The critical essay demonstrates:**	a comprehensive analysis of the effect of features of language/filmic techniques	a very clear analysis of the effect of features of language/filmic techniques	a clear analysis of the effect of features of language/filmic techniques	an adequate analysis of the effect of features of language/filmic techniques	limited analysis of the effect of features of language/filmic techniques	little analysis of features of language/filmic techniques	
Evaluation **The critical essay demonstrates:**	a committed, very clear evaluative stance with respect to the text and the task	a very clear evaluative stance with respect to the text and the task	a clear evaluative stance with respect to the text and the task	adequate evidence of an evaluative stance with respect to the text and the task	limited evidence of an evaluative stance with respect to the text and the task	little evidence of an evaluative stance with respect to the text and the task	

Technical Accuracy: Pass (20–10)

The critical essay demonstrates:

- few errors in spelling, grammar, sentence construction, punctuation and paragraphing
- the ability to be understood at first reading.

Technical Accuracy: Fail (9–0)

The critical essay demonstrates:

- errors in spelling, grammar, sentence construction, punctuation and paragraphing which impede understanding.

0 marks

- No knowledge of the text and its central concerns
- No attempt to answer the question and no textual evidence
- No analysis of features of language/filmic techniques
- No evidence of evaluation